Opening
Windows

OPENING WINDOWS

SPIRITUAL REFRESHMENT *for* YOUR WALK WITH CHRIST

MAX LUCADO, GARY SMALLEY
JONI EARECKSON TADA, SHEILA WALSH
CHUCK COLSON, CHARLES R. SWINDOLL
PHILIP YANCEY, MARILYN MEBERG
TONY EVANS, BILL HYBELS, AND MORE...

HOWARD BOOKS
A DIVISION OF SIMON & SCHUSTER
New York   London   Toronto   Sydney

Our purpose at Howard Books is to:
- *Increase* faith in the hearts of growing Christians
- *Inspire* holiness in the lives of believers
- *Instill* hope in the hearts of struggling people everywhere

Because He's coming again!

 Howard Books, a division of Simon & Schuster, Inc.
1230 Avenue of the Americas, New York, NY 10020
www.howardpublishing.com

10 Digit ISBN: 1-58229-676-6; 13 Digit ISBN: 978-1-58229-676-0
10 Digit ISBN: 1-4165-3782-1; 13 Digit ISBN: 978-1-4165-3782-3

10 9 8 7 6 5 4 3 2 1

HOWARD colophon is a registered trademark of Simon & Schuster, Inc.

Manufactured in the United States of America

For information regarding special discounts for bulk purchases, please contact Simon & Schuster Special Sales at 1-800-456-6798 or business@simonandschuster.com.

Compiled and edited by Mary Fairchild
Cover design by Torrey Sharp
Interior design by John Mark Luke Designs

CONTENTS

INTRODUCTION *by Max Lucado* ix

PART I: WINDOWS OF PRAISE AND WORSHIP

1. OPEN TO THE WONDER OF WORSHIP 3
   Reflection by Max Lucado

2. OPEN TO PRAISE IN ALL THINGS.......................11
   Reflection by Catherine Marshall

3. OPEN TO WORSHIP...17
   Reflection by Dennis Jernigan

4. OPEN TO PURE PRAISE......................................23
   Reflection by Jeff Walling

5. OPEN TO TOTAL HUMILITY 29
   Reflection by Sheila Walsh

6. OPEN TO SACRIFICE..35
   Reflection by Ravi Zacharias

7. OPEN TO HEAVENLY WORSHIP 41
   Reflection by Joni Eareckson Tada

Contents

Part 2: Windows of Prayer

8. Open to Constant Communication 49
Reflection by Thelma Wells

9. Open to Prayer in Faith 57
Reflection by Corrie ten Boom

10. Open to "Spiritual Therapy" 63
Reflection by Philip Yancey

11. Open to Life-Changing Prayer 69
Reflection by John Guest

12. Open to Emotion 75
Reflection by Charles R. Swindoll

13. Open to Prayer of the Heart 81
Reflection by Leanne Payne

14. Open to the Heart of God 87
Reflection by Cynthia Heald

15. Open to the Spirit's Leading 93
Reflection by Bill Hybels

16. Open to God's Communication 99
Reflection by Gary Smalley

Part 3: Windows of Wonder

17. Open to the Tug of a Child 107
Reflection by Jim McGuiggan

Contents

18. Open to the Mystery 113
Reflection by Elisabeth Elliot

19. Open to the Broken Body 119
Reflection by Paul Brand

20. Open to the "Second Look" 125
Reflection by Ken Gire

21. Open to the "Mirror of Life" 131
Reflection by Luci Shaw

22. Open to the Blessings of Sunset 137
Reflection by Wayne Watson

23. Open to Spontaneity 143
Reflection by Lloyd J. Ogilvie

PART 4: Windows of Grace

24. Open to Godly Grace 151
Reflection by Jerry Bridges

25. Open to the Good and Glad 157
Reflection by Marilyn Meberg

26. Open to Hospitality 163
Reflection by Miriam Huffman Rockness

27. Open to Faith and Freedom 169
Reflection by Gladys Hunt

28. Open to Childlike Rest 175
Reflection by Hannah Whitall Smith

Contents

PART 5: WINDOWS OF PURPOSE

29. OPEN TO GOD'S ALIGNMENT 183
    Reflection by Tony Evans

30. OPEN TO CLAIMING THE BEST........................ 191
    Refection by Calvin Miller

31. OPEN TO ADVENTURES WITH GOD 197
    Reflection by Valerie Bell

32. OPEN TO COMPASSIONATE MINISTRY.............. 203
    Reflection by Warren Wiersbe

33. OPEN TO JOYFUL WITNESS 209
    Reflection by Tim Stafford

34. OPEN TO HOLY WITNESS 215
    Reflection by Charles Colson

35. OPEN TO GODLY PASSION 223
    Reflection by Larry Crabb Jr.

CLOSING PRAYER *by Max Lucado* 229

CONTRIBUTORS.. 231

ACKNOWLEDGMENTS 239

INTRODUCTION

MAX LUCADO

Imagine yourself in a dark room. It is daylight outside, but it is dark within. The windows are closed, the drapes are drawn, the shutters closed tight. The room yields no light. You fumble your way around the room, but progress is slow and the path is painful. Stubbed toes, scraped knees, skinned shins: it is hard to walk in a dark room.

Just as hard as it is to walk in a dark world. Many try and many are wounded as a result, tripping over their problems, bumping into one another in the shadows, walking into walls. No wonder the world is so full of pain. We are insecure because we can't see who we are. We are unsure because we don't know where we are going. But every so often a beam of light slices through the blackness. A curtain is drawn, a window is raised, and a shaft of light penetrates the darkness. What was dark is now bright; what was opaque is now clear. What was stale is now fresh.

What a difference.

When the light comes in, peace comes in. Moments before, our steps were timid. Now there is a sureness to our step, a confidence to move through the corridors of light opening one window after another. Why? Because once we've walked in the light, we don't want to walk in the darkness anymore. Amazingly, this peace, this confidence, began with the single gesture of opening windows.

What are these windows? The windows of prayer and praise. Praise opens the window of our hearts, preparing us to walk more closely with God. Prayer raises the window of our spirit, enabling us to listen more clearly to the Father.

Choose to leave the windows closed and the curtains shut, and you choose to live in a cold, dark world. Choose to open the windows of praise and prayer, and you allow your Father to bring light and warmth into your world.

So—throw back the curtain, and see His light. Open the window and hear His voice. Raise the glass, and feel the gentle breeze of the Holy Spirit. Allow your world to be warmed and illuminated.

As you open windows of prayer and praise, remember this holy promise: "I will open the windows of heaven for you" (Malachi 3:10 NLT).

PART I

WINDOWS OF
PRAISE AND WORSHIP

THE MOMENT IS MAGICAL. IT IS LINDBERGH SPOTTING THE LAND THROUGH THE CLOUDS.

"If you knew the gift of God and who it is that asks you for a drink, you would have asked him and he would have given you living water."

JOHN 4:10

CHAPTER 1

OPEN TO THE
WONDER OF WORSHIP

Reflection
MAX LUCADO

She comes to the well at noon. Why? Why not at dawn as did the other women? Doesn't make sense unless it was the other women she sought to avoid. Maybe the heat of the sun was more bearable than the heat of their gossip. So she comes to the well at noon.

But today she's not alone. A stranger sits at the base of the well, legs outstretched, eyes closed. Face moist from the heat. The woman looks around and sees no one else. When she looks back, His eyes are open and looking at her. Embarrassed, she turns away.

He stands and asks her for a drink of water.

Her response is salty with distrust, "You are a Jew and I am a Samaritan woman. How can you ask me for a drink?" (John 4:9). The woman has reason to be cautious. She knows what men really mean when they ask for favors. The wall is up. Jesus removes the top brick.

"If you only knew the free gift of God and who it is that is asking you for water, you would have asked him, and he would have given you living water" (verse 10 NCV).

No lecture. No speeches. No homilies on how far He had come to help. No finger-pointing at her past. None of that. Just an appeal. An appeal for trust. . . .

"If only you knew that I have come to help and not condemn. If only you knew that tomorrow will be better than today. If only you knew the gift I have brought: eternal life—endless, tearless, graveless life . . . if only you knew."

The woman is slow to trust. . . .

The high sun casts short shadows of the two. She still holds her jug. He still holds her attention. "Whoever drinks the water I give will never be thirsty. The water I give will become a spring of water gushing up inside that person, giving eternal life" (verse 14 NCV).

The words connect. She pilgrims a parched desert. Face furrowed. Eyes searching. Endless sage and sorrow. Every oasis a wavy mirage. Five times love pledged. Five times love failed. She's been thirsty so long.

"Sir, give me this water so I will never be thirsty again" (verse 15 NCV).

Now she removes a few bricks. Her distrust still

great, her desperation still greater . . . she's willing to take the risk.

So is Jesus. But one wall still stands. There is one obstacle remaining. The teacher gently invites her to dismantle it. "Go get your husband and come back here" (verse 16 NCV).

She winces at the words. *My husband? My husband! I don't want to talk about my husband. Talk to me about water. About eternal life. Talk to me about anything but the part of my life that hurts the most.*

She looks into the eyes of this Jew and wonders what is behind them. *He is different. He doesn't treat me like other Jews. He doesn't look at me like other men.* She could change the subject. She could ignore the question. She could lie. But none of that seems right. So she removes what remains of the wall between them.

"I have no husband" (verse 17).

Read slowly Jesus's response. "You are right to say you have no husband. Really you have had five husbands, and the man you live with now is not your husband. You told the truth" (verse 17–18 NCV).

That's all Jesus seeks. That we tell the truth. That we come out of hiding. An encounter with Christ is midnight at the masquerade. Time to remove the mask.

And so she does. With the walls down and the mask off, she entrusts Him with her deepest yearning.

"Sir, I can see that you are a prophet. Our ancestors worshiped on this mountain, but you [Jews] say that Jerusalem is the place where people must worship" (verses 19–20 NCV).

Don't misinterpret what the woman is doing with this question.

She's not avoiding Jesus; she's inviting Jesus. She's not closing up; she's opening up. She's escorting this teacher up to the edge of the darkest cave in her world and asking Him if he has a candle.

Let me tell you where I really hurt, she is saying. *Let me tell you what keeps me awake at night. Not the rejection. I'm used to being lonely. I can stand having no husband. What I cannot stand is not knowing where God is. Can You tell me?*

Pain distills the deep questions. . . .

There in the shadow of the well of Sychar, to a rejected woman, God explains the mystery of worship.

He tells her that a day is coming when the place of worship won't make any difference. A time is coming and has come when the *where* and the *when* of worship will not matter. What matters is the heart. . . .

When the woman heard this—she smiled. She knew what Jesus meant, and she told Him. "I know that the Messiah is coming. . . . When the Messiah comes, he will explain everything to us" (verse 25 NCV).

The moment is magical.

It's Lindbergh spotting the land through the

clouds. It's Handel pounding on his piano the final measure of *Messiah*. . . .

It's the Messiah finding a Messiah-seeker.

It's the definition of *worship*. A hungry heart finding the Father's feast. A searching soul finding the Father's face. A wandering pilgrim spotting the Father's house. Finding God. Finding God seeking us. This is worship. This is a worshiper.

YOUR FRESH TAKE

Have you ever been surprised to "meet Jesus" in a place or situation where you were trying to avoid or escape some unpleasantness? What happened?_____

_____

_____

_____

_____

Consider your own spiritual journey. Who do you sense "removes the bricks" that separate you from God? _____

_____

_____

_____

_____

In your own words describe "the mystery of worship." Use your own metaphors: It's like . . .

_____

_____

_____

_____

_____

_____

_____

8

Lord, as I Open . . .

THE WINDOWS OF MY LIFE TO YOU—EVEN IF JUST
A CRACK—MAKE YOUR PRESENCE REAL. SHOW ME
THE MEANING OF TRUE WORSHIP. THROUGH JESUS I
PRAY, AMEN.

ALL THESE SMALL ACTS PUT
TOGETHER—LITTLE TRICKLES
OF PRAISE—WERE RUNNING
TOGETHER, BEGINNING TO
FORM A RIVER OF PRAISE.

*Give thanks in all circumstances, for this is
God's will for you in Christ Jesus.*

1 THESSALONIANS 5:18

CHAPTER 2

OPEN TO
PRAISE IN ALL THINGS

Reflection
CATHERINE MARSHALL

Yesterday morning in my prayer time, God showed me that if I wanted more vitality for my work hours, I had to deal with the following resentments that were smoldering inside me.

I resent my lack of social graces in certain situations, which I'm inclined to blame on my childhood years when I too often fled social encounters.

I resent the fact that I'm such a poor sleeper. I can see that resentment produces tension and, of course, accumulated tension through the day is one reason I'm not sleeping better.

Here at Evergreen Farm there are so many stairs to climb, and outside, hills and more hills, which I cannot mount because of my breathlessness. This condition is a constant embarrassment and the central thorn in my flesh. I resent my damaged lungs.

I see this morning that there are deeper resentments

still: that of creeping old age, being progressively shut down, as it were, and, of course, out there—death. Have I not always resented the fact of death, even though I have total belief in and expectancy about the life after death?

How can I come to terms with all this?

The answer came in 1 Thessalonians 5:18. I am to praise God for *all* things, regardless of where they seem to originate. Doing this, He points out, is the key to receiving the blessings of God. Praise will wash away my resentments. I've known this, accepted it, even written about praise. But as I began praising Him yesterday, my efforts were wooden.

Then came these thoughts: I was to ignore my feelings and act on the principle. I was to do it despite the lack of joy—simply because God told me to. True praise grows out of the recognition and acknowledgment that in His time God will bring good out of bad. There is the intolerable situation on the one hand and the fulfillment of Romans 8:28 on the other hand. ("All things work together for good . . ." KJV) By an act of will and through imagination and with faith, I am to turn my back on the bad and face the good, and begin actively to praise God for it as Scripture commands.

Shortly after this insight my cleaning woman called in to say that she was not coming. Praised God for this, though mechanically.

Following that, joy began spilling over into the

tiny everydayness of my life. Walked by a vase of beautiful roses from our garden and buried my nose in the fragrance, saying, "Praise You, Lord, for such beauty!"

Stepped onto our patio for a moment to listen to the birds singing. "Praise You, Lord, for all Your creatures."

Then came the feeling that all these small acts put together—little trickles of praise—were running together, beginning to form a river of praise.

Continued to praise God for *all* things, good and bad. All setbacks, frustrations, and resentments.

Praise You, Lord, for my awkwardness in certain social situations.

Praise You, Lord, that I have trouble sleeping.

Praise You, Lord, for my weak lungs.

Praise You, Lord, for creeping old age.

Praise You, Lord, for the death that comes to all of us.

This morning I actually woke up with praise swelling in my heart. Only later did I realize I had slept through the entire night! Cannot remember when I last did this! Awakened by the coffeepot going on. Imagine! Praise God indeed!

YOUR FRESH TAKE

Here most of Catherine Marshall's resentments are not complaints about other people but about her own inadequacies. Answering honestly, what personal limitations do you resent? _____

_____

_____

_____

_____

Try to turn your limitations to praise. (Think in terms of praising God "in" all things if not "for" all things.) What else might you need to do to "turn [your] back on the bad and face the good"? _____

_____

_____

_____

_____

Try full-tilt praise for one day, and see if you agree that "little trickles" flow together and form a "river of praise."

Lord, I Open . . .

MY HEART, WANTING TO TURN THE PERSONAL
LIMITATIONS AND THORNS THAT I RESENT INTO
PRAISE OF YOU. I ASK YOU TO ACCEPT MY PRAISE
AND LIGHTEN MY SPIRIT AS I AWAIT THE FULFILLMENT
OF YOUR GOOD WILL. IN THE NAME OF JESUS, AMEN.

THE BEAUTY OF ANY RELATIONSHIP
THAT BEARS FRUIT AND LIFE IS
THAT IT IS ENTERED INTO OF AND
BY ONE'S OWN CHOICE.

Ascribe to the LORD the glory due his name;
worship the LORD in the splendor of his holiness.

PSALM 29:2

CHAPTER 3

OPEN TO WORSHIP

Reflection
DENNIS JERNIGAN

Worship begins with *trust*. Trust means presenting our hearts to God and saying, "Lord, here I am. I cannot see You clearly, for the dust of this life has settled on the glass of my heart and I see You only faintly. Would You please take me to Yourself and wipe off that dust so that I might see You and know You a little better?" Worship is trusting God enough to let Him take your heart and cleanse it—free it—of anything that separates you from Him.

Worship continues with *honesty*. . . .

Honesty is the basis of my relationship with Christ. Even when I don't hear His voice or understand His ways as I would like—even then—I can be honest with God and trust that He will not "write me off" or consider me a hopeless case!

At a practical level, worship is simply *obedience* to God. Obedience requires surrender of our wills to the truth of His will. Giving up my will does not mean a loss of personal identity, as we see in the practice of many cults. Obedience, and our subsequent surrender, follows our recognition of our complete need of Him.

Worship is also a matter of *choice*. It's true that God's Word *commands* us to praise Him and worship Him, yet God does not force us to love Him. The beauty of any relationship that bears fruit and life is that it is entered into of and by one's own choice. God chose me. And He allows me the freedom to choose Him in return. Yet, because of the holiness of God, we know that one day every knee will bow and every tongue will confess that He is Lord. That is reality simply because He is God. But God never forces us to *love* Him.

So why do we have verses that command us to love and worship Him? I believe it is because He provided the law (His commandments) as a teacher that guides us to the truth. Ultimately, we need God, and we need to know Him. Like parents who command their children to do their homework because they know they will need that knowledge to succeed in corporate life, so, too, our Father blessed us with His law because He knew we would need to know Him if we were to truly succeed at life! He commanded us: "Love the LORD your God with all your heart and with all your soul and with all your strength" (Deuteronomy 6:5; see also Mark 12:30).

Further, worship is an act of *confession* and, therefore, healing. "Confess your sins to each other and pray for each other so that you may be healed. The prayer of a righteous man is powerful and effective" (James 5:16).

How does confession bring healing? If I went to a physician seeking healing for a certain ailment but would not tell him where I hurt, how could I be healed? Confession is not for the doctor but for the patient! Yes, God knows where we hurt, but do we trust God (the Great Physician) enough to allow ourselves to be vulnerable to His healing? Sin is the ultimate ailment. When the "cells" of our heart have been rid of the "germs" of sin by the "antibiotics" of redeeming blood, life is no longer hampered and the flow of relationship is once again restored—and healing of the soul takes place.

Do you see how confession is simply one more facet of worship? If we desire a healthy relationship with our Creator, then, as with our physical bodies, we must feed our souls with the proper diet: a diet of relationship through confession, praise, and worship.

Finally, worship is *drawing others to Christ*—and this, too, has to do with confession—confession of our faith in Christ. When Christ is lifted up, He draws others to Himself (see John 12:32).

YOUR FRESH TAKE

Trust. Honesty. Obedience. Choice. Confession. Drawing others to Christ. Which of these facets of worship is easiest for you to engage in? _____

_____

_____

_____

Which facet is hardest for you? Why? _____

_____

_____

_____

_____

Do you think each facet builds upon the previous, in the order presented by Dennis Jernigan? If not, how do you think worship works? _____

_____

_____

_____

_____

Discuss the relationship between choosing to worship and being commanded to worship. _____

_____

_____

_____

_____

Lord, I Open . . .

MY HEART AND SOUL TO YOU, TRUSTING YOU, CHOOSING TO LOVE YOU. HAVE MERCY ON ME, LORD, AS I LOOK TO YOU FOR HEALING, FOR RESTORATION. ACCEPT MY PRAISE AND WORSHIP. IN THE NAME OF JESUS, AMEN.

MAINTAINING A FOCUS ON GOD

WILL TAKE OUR PRAISE

TO HEIGHTS THAT

NOTHING ELSE CAN.

*Let us run with perseverance the race marked
out for us. Let us fix our eyes on Jesus,
the author and perfecter of our faith.*

HEBREWS 12:1–2

CHAPTER 4

OPEN TO
PURE PRAISE

Reflection
JEFF WALLING

Training the eyes of our heart on God will free our dancing [with God] in more ways than one. First, keeping your eyes solidly on your dance partner keeps you from being distracted by onlookers. Hebrews contains an image that illustrates this well.

The New Testament letter to the Hebrews is an epistle of encouragement. Written to Jewish believers who were trying to hang on to their newfound faith, it gives advice on maintaining your direction in the face of critical opposition. The famous metaphor of the Christian race found in the twelfth chapter contains a command that's critical to dancing with God: "Therefore, since we are surrounded by such a great cloud of witnesses, let us throw off everything that hinders and the sin that so easily entangles, and let us run with perseverance the race marked out for us. Let us fix our eyes on Jesus, the author and perfecter of our faith" (Hebrews 12:1–2).

The writer pictures a stadium filled with spectators watching us run the race of faith. The witnesses he refers to may be angels or saints from years gone by. Some imagine Moses and Joshua sitting next to Noah and Jacob munching popcorn and cheering us on from the stands. While their presence may be motivating, notice that the writer never tells us to look at the spectators. Quite the opposite. After commanding us to strip off anything that might hold us back from running freely toward God—a directive that strangely reminds one of David stripping down to his linen ephod—he tells us to "fix our eyes on Jesus."

While the crowd pictured in Hebrews 12 may be an encouraging one, the crowds that surround us on earth aren't always so. But whether our crowd cheers or boos us, we must keep our gaze locked on Christ's loving face. It makes sense. The fickle crowd can easily distract or dishearten. One minute they love you, and the next they're calling for the coach to pull you from the game. Not so with Jesus. He always pulls for you. His eyes are always filled with hope. Like the apostle Peter walking on the water, we'll not sink as long as our eyes are on Him.

Second, maintaining a focus on God will take our praise to heights that nothing else can. I have heard it suggested that exuberant praise is a great witness to the nonbeliever. And though I can't agree more, I must never allow my focus to shift from praising God because He is great to praising God because it will attract or influence others. Not only would that corrupt the purity of my motive for praise, it would divert my attention from the source of my passion. What greater motive for praise is there than the great mercy of God? . . .

Through the years I've tried several methods of calming nervous grooms, but there's only one that's literally "fool" proof. I just say, "Will you repeat these words after me as you look into the eyes of your bride." It never fails. When his eyes meet hers, all other thoughts flee. . . .

Third, keeping our eyes on God will meter our praise better than any human judge. If I am earnestly channeling my praise straight to Him, His overwhelming holiness and purity will keep my exuberance in balance. If I do begin to dance out of step with Him, it will quickly be evident. His righteousness will leave no room for my impropriety. As John declares, "God is light; in him there is no darkness at all" (1 John 1:5). If I look with commitment on His goodness, I will have little trouble keeping my praise pure.

YOUR FRESH TAKE

Have there been times in your worship when you were more aware of surrounding spectators than of Jesus? What was the effect of your lack of focus?

_____

_____

_____

Consider Jeff Walling's observation about "the fickle crowd": "One minute they love you, and the next they're calling for the coach to pull you from the game. Not so with Jesus." Have you found this contrast to be true? List examples of the faithfulness of God, even when other people turned away. _____

_____

_____

_____

Is it easier to keep your focus on Jesus in seasons of "want" or in seasons of "plenty"? Why? _____

_____

_____

_____

How could your motive for praise become corrupt? How can you keep your praise pure? _____

_____

_____

Lord, I Open . . .

MY EYES TO GAZE UPON YOU, LIKE A GROOM OR BRIDE AT A WEDDING, ABSORBED IN THE LOVE OF MY LIFE, NOT ON THE SURROUNDING CROWD OF WITNESSES. I WANT TO BE A POSITIVE MODEL FOR OTHER PEOPLE, BUT, LORD, HELP ME TO FOCUS ON YOU. ALLOW ME TO KNOW THE BENEFITS THAT COME FROM KEEPING MY PRAISE PURE. THROUGH JESUS I PRAY, AMEN.

THE FORMULAS WERE BARREN TO
ME UNTIL I BEGAN LITERALLY
TO PROSTRATE MYSELF ON THE
FLOOR BEFORE THE LORD.

Come, let us bow down in worship, let us kneel
before the LORD our Maker; for he is our God
and we are the people of his pasture.

PSALM 95:6–7

CHAPTER 5

OPEN TO
TOTAL HUMILITY

Reflection
SHEILA WALSH

As I sat in the church service, I was moved by the atmosphere of worship. Even the teenage boys were singing with all their hearts. *This is a special place*, I thought.

. . . [The pastor's] message was simple and startling to me. Like so many of the most powerful truths in the world, the kernel was simple truth. His message was taken from Matthew's Gospel, a story I have known since childhood, and yet I heard it that day as if the ink were not yet dry on the manuscript.

A man with leprosy came and knelt before him and said, "Lord, if you are willing, you can make me clean."

Jesus reached out his hand and touched the man. "I am willing," he said. "Be clean!" Immediately he was cured of his leprosy. (Matthew 8:2–3)

Matthew says that multitudes were following Jesus wherever He went, but there was something different about this man, even apart from his leprosy. The Greek word used here for *knelt* is from the root "to worship," to kneel down and lick someone's hand like a dog, in total humility. I'm sure that there were many needs present in the crowd that day, but the one who received his miracle was the man who humbled himself and knelt at the feet of Christ and worshiped, saying, "If you are willing, you can make me clean."

In bed that night I thought about that for a long time. How can we appropriate the faith and humility of this man? So many of us go to great lengths to follow the "latest move" of God. We make sure we attend the right conventions and read all the right books; we are "with Christ," part of the "in" crowd. But I think God asks us simply to fall at His feet and worship, to acknowledge that we cannot heal ourselves, that we are dependent on Him every moment. Going deeper in our lives with God is a more solitary life. I am committed to community. It is the church, it is our calling, but it is only as we are real with God and broken before Him that we have anything to bring to one another.

I used to try and find a perfect formula to worship at home. I would get out a hymn book and sing my way through many of the great hymns of the faith.

Or I would work with a book of liturgy. I would sing worship choruses until my cat hid under the bed, but the formulas were barren to me until I began literally to prostrate myself on the floor before the Lord, confessing my weakness and sinfulness. Now as I meditate on the goodness of God, I find myself singing or weeping or laughing. Worshiping God.

I have no ten steps to offer you, but I do encourage you to follow the lead of a leper and fall at the feet of Jesus and worship Him. We are called to be a home for God, a prepared room where He can live and pour out His life and love.

YOUR FRESH TAKE

What worship or prayer "formulas" have you tried that have been "barren" to you? Why are such formulas so empty? _____

_____

_____

_____

Imagine yourself being in the presence of Jesus Himself. What about Him—and what about you—would make you willing and able to prostrate yourself before Him?

_____

_____

_____

_____

How would being broken before God and admitting that you cannot heal yourself change your worship and your approach to God and to life? _____

_____

_____

_____

_____

Lord, as I Open . . .

MYSELF TO YOU IN HUMBLE CONFESSION AND
WORSHIP, I ASK THAT YOU MAKE MY SPIRIT CLEAN.
AMEN.

DOES THE WORLD GET OUR BEST
WHILE GOD MERELY
GETS THE LEFTOVERS?

When you bring injured, crippled or diseased
animals and offer them as sacrifices, should I
accept them from your hands?

MALACHI 1:13

CHAPTER 6

OPEN TO SACRIFICE

Reflection
RAVI ZACHARIAS

It is impossible to worship without sacrifice, the giving of our best. But the people had begun to show contempt for God by bringing the lame and the blind and the sick of their fold and giving their leftovers to God as their worship.

When I was about twelve or thirteen years old, I was asked by our Sunday-school teacher if I would be willing to play Joseph in the nativity mime that Christmas. I must add as kindly but as truthfully as I can that the church itself was so rankly liberal that the gospel was lost under the weight of ceremony. I was on the verge of saying no to this request, for I really did not know what all that meant. But then I was told what I would need to do: basically, to walk Mary to the altar with her arm in mine, stand there, turn around, have her put her arm in mine again, and walk out. No words, no big acting skill

35

needed. When I met who was going to play Mary, I decided this would be quite a thrill.

I arrived at the church early and was walking around with time to kill. On a table at the altar, I saw a silver bowl with wafers in it. Having very little knowledge of what this could be, I took a handful of those wafers and enjoyed them as I admired all the great art and statuary in that fine cathedral. Suddenly I saw the vicar coming out of the vestry and walking straight toward me. I politely greeted him and continued my enjoyment of the biscuits in hand. He stopped, stared, and quite out of control, shouted, "What are you doing?"

As surprised by his outburst as he was at my activity, I said, "I am Joseph in the nativity mime."

That evidently was not what he was asking. "What is that in your hand?" he demanded. As he stared me down from head to toe, he could see that there was more in my pocket too. I received the most incomprehensible tongue-lashing to which I had ever been subjected. The word that the priest kept repeating was the word *sacrilege*. I chose never to check out its meaning, for I was sure this was the end of the line for me, having done something I did not even know how to pronounce.

Years later I could not help but chuckle when I was reading G. Campbell Morgan's definition of *sacrilege*. He said that it is normally defined as taking something that belongs to God and using it profanely.

We all know the instance in the Book of Daniel when Belshaazar took the vessels in the temple and used them for his night of carousing and blasphemy. That was a sacrilegious use. But sacrilege, said Morgan, does not only consist of such profane use. In its worst form it consists of taking something and giving it to God when it means absolutely nothing to you. That was the charge God brought against His people when He said, "You bring the lame and the blind and the sick as an offering, is that not wrong?" (see Malachi 1:8).

Worship at its core is a giving to God of all that is your best. This cannot be done without the sacrifice of the acclaim and adulation of the world. If we were to only pause for a few moments and take stock, we would see how close we all come to sacrilege each day.

Do we give Him the best of our time?

Do we give Him the best of our energies?

Do we give Him the best of our thinking?

Do we give Him the best of our wealth?

Do we give Him the best of our dreams and plans?

Or does the world get our best while God merely gets the leftovers?

YOUR FRESH TAKE

Think about the following categories: your (1) time, (2) energies, (3) thinking, (4) wealth, and (5) dreams and plans. What would it mean for you to give God your best, rather than your "leftovers"? _____

_____

_____

_____

_____

How is giving God something that costs us nothing an even greater sacrilege than Belshaazar's profane use of the temple vessels? _____

_____

_____

_____

_____

Read Romans 12:1 and Hebrews 13:15–16. Under the heading "My Worship and Praise," write a summary sentence describing what these scriptures say about a pleasing sacrifice and what they mean to you.

_____

_____

_____

_____

Lord, I Open . . .

MY "BEST" TO YOU—AS IMPERFECT AS IT MAY BE. I
OFFER THIS TO YOU OUT OF LOVE AND GRATITUDE
FOR YOUR SACRIFICE FOR ME. RECEIVE MY GIFT,
MY LIVING SACRIFICE, MY PRAISE. THROUGH JESUS
I COME, AMEN.

THIS OTHER PLACE OF WONDERFUL

BEAUTY WAS PRESENT ALL

THE TIME. ONLY INCHES AWAY.

*To him who sits on the throne and to the
Lamb be praise and honor and glory and
power, for ever and ever!*

REVELATION 5:13

CHAPTER 7

OPEN TO
HEAVENLY WORSHIP

Reflection
JONI EARECKSON TADA

Heaven is close. Perhaps closer than we imagine.

It's a little like saying to an unborn infant in his mother's womb, "Do you realize that you are about to be born into a great big world full of mountains, rivers, and a sun and a moon? In fact, you exist in that wonderful world right now."

"Wait a minute," the unborn baby might say. "No way. My world is the one surrounding me. It's soft, warm, and dark. You'll never convince me that just a few hairbreadths outside this uterus exists this place of rivers, mountains, and a sun and moon, whatever that stuff is."

Dear baby! There he is, safe in his little world, ignorant of the fact that a more glorious world is enclosing and encasing his. A world for which he is being fashioned. Only when he is birthed into it will he comprehend that all along his warm, dark world was within it. This other place of wonderful beauty was present all the time. Only inches away. . . .

[In heaven we will] worship with the angels. They've had a lot of practice at worshiping, as well as access to heaven's throne. They've seen it all. Yet when we arrive in heaven, it will be *their* privilege to worship with us. Just think what our worship will sound like. In Revelation 5:11–13, angels crowd before the throne, "numbering thousands upon thousands, and ten thousand times ten thousand. . . . In a loud voice they sang: 'Worthy is the Lamb, who was slain, to receive power and wealth and wisdom and strength and honor and glory and praise!'"

Every time I read that verse, I recall a marvelous experience at the Moody Pastors' Conference. I was told that the singing would be out of this world. And it was. When I wheeled onto the platform and parked near Dr. Joe Stowell and the other speakers, I scanned the auditorium of 1,800 men and got the jolt of my life. Somehow it escaped me that I would be amongst so many, many men.

The song leader had the men stand up, spread out into the aisles, and fill the stage. When they held hymn books high and broke into a rousing chorus, a jet blast of sound hit me head-on. A pastor held a hymnal close so I could sing along, but I only managed half the first verse. Something forced me to stop, close my eyes, and just listen.

Never had I been so utterly surrounded by sound.

It was pure and powerful, clear and deep, enveloping me, resonating through my bones, and shaking the chair in which I sat. A thunderous waterfall of perfect bass and baritone, so passionate it made my heart break.

Through tears I tried to join in the second verse, but my wispy soprano voice sounded thin and frail. I was a tiny leaf carried helplessly along a surging current, spilling over and splashing with joy, all joy and music. It was a moment of ecstasy, so serendipitous and God-anointed, that I had to step outside myself and be carried heavenward. I could do nothing but laugh through my tears and enjoy the ride. If this earthly choir moved me, how much more when our voices blend with the angels!

YOUR FRESH TAKE

Acknowledging that here in this world our awareness of heaven is limited (somewhat like a baby in a
womb), describe what you think heaven will be like.
Base your description on Scripture and on "the best"
of God's design of this world. _____

_____

_____

_____

_____

What three songs do you want to sing in heaven?
Why are they meaningful to you? _____

_____

_____

_____

_____

Martin Luther said, "The devil does not stay where
music is." Discuss a time when music seemed to usher
you into the presence of God. _____

_____

_____

_____

_____

Lord, as I Open . . .

MY MOUTH TO SING YOUR PRAISES, OPEN MY
SPIRITUAL EYES TO THE PRESENCE OF YOUR KINGDOM
HERE ON EARTH AND WHET MY APPETITE FOR
THE EXPANSIVE OTHERWORLDLY KINGDOM I WILL
SOMEDAY ENJOY FOREVER. AMEN.

PART 2

WINDOWS OF PRAYER

PRAYING CONTINUALLY INVOLVES
ABIDING IN THE FATHER'S
PRESENCE, WHETHER
FORMAL PRAYERS ARE
UTTERED OR NOT.

Be joyful always; pray continually.
1 THESSALONIANS 5:16–17

CHAPTER 8

OPEN TO
CONSTANT COMMUNICATION

Reflection
THELMA WELLS

I love to pray. I guess I'd better since I spend most of my time doing it. I wake up in the morning praying. I pray in the tub; I pray while I wash clothes or water the grass; I pray when I'm talking on the phone or hugging my children or driving or exercising; I pray in meetings and during business negotiations; I pray on airplanes; I pray for the sick and the suffering and for people I don't know. You get the picture. In almost every situation my mouth isn't moving, but my brain is grooving. In my mind I pray all the time.

One day as I was hugging my son good-bye after a visit, he said to me, "You're praying for me again, aren't you?" I looked a bit startled because I hadn't *said* a word. I nodded my head yes. He said, "You're always praying. I can tell. You've done that since we were little. We all know it. But that's good, Mama. That's good. Thank you. Keep it up; don't stop now."

. . . I tend to pray when there's no apparent reason to pray. I just love to fellowship with my heavenly Father.

Some of my prayers sound like this:

- "Lord, have mercy."

- "Help me, Lord."

- "Thank You, Jesus."

- "Speak to my heart, Lord."

- "Lord, are You listening?" . . .

- "God, why are You so slow?"

- "What's this all about, Jesus?"

- "Do You hear me, Lord?"

- "Am I supposed to keep asking You to do this, Sir?"

- "Look, Lord, I need an answer!"

- "Praise the name of Jesus."

- "I love You, Lord."

Some of those prayers may sound as if I'm a little sassy with God or disrespectful of Him, but the truth is, God is my Father and yours. He knows all about us. We can come boldly to Him, and He will understand exactly what we mean and the attitude with which we mean it. In other words, we can come clean with God. I don't know how your prayers sound, but I'm glad God can read our minds and know our hearts. When we realize that prayer is simply expressing the heart's sincere desire to God, in silence or aloud, prayer can become as natural as breathing.

When I'm in an attitude of prayer all the time, it's pretty hard to worry or to think of negative or evil things. People have asked me why I'm so happy all the time. I may not always be so happy, but I have the joy, joy, joy, joy down in my heart! Such joy can come only in the presence of the Lord. It's a joy that brings contentment when things are topsy-turvy. It's a joy that calms my fears and smooths my feathers and gives me peace when trials and tribulations are on the rampage. That joy surpasses all understanding as I trust in my Friend and Companion, Jesus.

Have you prayed today? Wherever you are and whatever you're doing, right now is a good time. You don't have to use any theological or flowery words. Just be yourself; He'll understand exactly what you mean.

If you don't talk to Him every day, why not start now and make it a habit to talk to Him whenever you think about it? That must have been how I started:

just communicating with Him silently whenever He came to my mind. I think that's what Paul, Silas, and Timothy meant when they urged the Thessalonians to "pray without ceasing" (1 Thessalonians 5:17 NKJV). Praying continually involves abiding in the Father's presence, whether formal prayers are uttered or not.

God created us to have fellowship with Him. When you make a habit of talking to Him often, you'll make Him happy and He'll make you content. There is joy in the presence of the Lord.

YOUR FRESH TAKE

Identify two or three times in your daily schedule when you pray. How did prayer become part of your normal routine at these times? _____

_____

_____

Identify two or three times in your daily schedule when you are least aware of God. What conscious changes can you make to increase your awareness of God in these parts of your day? (Consider any insights or implications from your answer to the previous question.)

_____

_____

How would your day change if God were the first thing you thought of when waking in the morning and the last thing on your mind before sleeping?

_____

_____

_____

Do people who are important to you know you are praying for them? If not, what will you do to assure them of your prayers? _____

_____

_____

_____

Lord, I Open . . .

MY MIND AND HEART TO YOU. I WANT TO KEEP
PRAYING AND TALKING TO YOU—BRINGING EVERY
BIT OF MY LIFE BEFORE YOU, SEEKING YOUR COUNSEL,
HEARING YOUR CORRECTION, AND ASKING YOUR
BLESSING. INCREASE THE JOY OF THE LORD IN MY
HEART. I PRAISE YOUR NAME. AMEN.

THERE IS A VAST DIFFERENCE
BETWEEN PRAYER IN FAITH
AND FAITH IN PRAYER.

*When the Son of Man comes, will he
find faith on the earth?*

LUKE 18:8

CHAPTER 9

OPEN TO
PRAYER IN FAITH

Reflection
CORRIE TEN BOOM

When Betsie and I were in Ravensbruck, she became very ill. I took her to the prison hospital, and she asked me, "Corrie, please pray with me. Ask the Lord Jesus to heal me. He has said, 'If you shall lay hands upon the sick they shall be healed.' Please do that for me."

I prayed and laid hands on her, and both Betsie and I trusted the Lord for healing. The next morning, I ran from the barracks and looked through the window of the hospital and found Betsie's bed was empty. I ran from window to window, until I finally saw her body. They were getting ready to take it to the crematorium. It was the darkest moment of my life.

Then, just a few days later, I was summoned to the prison office. For some reason I was being released from prison. Surely it was a clerical error, but whatever the cause, I was free to go. It was a miracle of God.

When I came to the office, I discovered nobody

there knew that Betsie was dead. So I asked, "Is my sister also free?"

"No. She stays here until the end of the war."

"Can I stay with her?"

The official became furious and shouted at me. "Disappear! Get out of here!"

Suddenly I saw God's side of what had happened. Suppose Betsie had gotten better and I had to leave her behind? I would have been forced to return to Holland and leave her alone in that horrible camp. I could not have stood it. But she had been released from the concentration camp and was now enjoying all the glory of heaven. I walked out of the camp that day praising and thanking the Lord for that unanswered prayer. Yet it really wasn't unanswered. It was answered in God's way, not mine.

So often we pray and then fret anxiously, waiting for God to hurry up and do something. All the while God is waiting for us to calm down, so He can do something through us.

There is a vast difference between prayer in faith and faith in prayer. Faith in prayer is very common. Prayer in faith is so uncommon that our Lord questions if He will find any of it on earth when He comes back (see Luke 18:8). Prayer in faith is a commanded duty; it is always reverently making known our requests unto God in full confidence that, if we ask anything according to His will, He hears us; and that according to our faith, an answer to our prayers will be granted us.

Praying in faith comes from an abiding faith in the Person prayed to—the confidence is in Him. It is based on a knowledge of who He is, and on a trusted conviction that He is worthy to be trusted. Praying in faith is the act of a simple-hearted child of God. Can we teach ourselves to pray in faith? We can indeed train ourselves, but the joyful experience is that it is the Spirit of God who does the job. So give room in your heart for the Holy Spirit.

YOUR FRESH TAKE

Think about your attitudes toward prayer. Do you practice "prayer in faith" or "faith in prayer"?

_____

_____

_____

_____

Remember a time when you were "fretting," waiting for God to act. Can you now see that He might have been waiting for you to calm down so He could act through you? How can this reflection of past experience help change your prayer patterns in the future? _____

_____

_____

_____

_____

Thank God for one time when hindsight shows you that He, by His grace, did not "do it your way." In what ways can this hindsight change your praying patterns? (Consider Luke 22:42.) _____

_____

_____

_____

_____

Lord, as I Open . . .

MYSELF, IN CONFIDENCE, TO YOU AND YOUR HOLY
SPIRIT, SHOW ME AGAIN THAT YOU ARE WORTHY OF
MY TRUST. SHOW ME THAT YOU ARE A FAITHFUL AND
LOVING FATHER WANTING ONLY THE BEST FOR ME
AND ALL YOUR CHILDREN. THROUGH JESUS, AMEN.

I HAVE A SNEAKING SUSPICION THAT
DAVID WROTE PSALMS AS A
FORM OF SPIRITUAL THERAPY.

*I will take refuge in the shadow of your
wings until the disaster has passed.*

PSALM 57:1

CHAPTER 10

OPEN TO
"SPIRITUAL THERAPY"

Reflection
PHILIP YANCEY

If you read the psalms attributed to David and then try to envision his life, you will fail miserably. You might imagine a pious, otherworldly hermit, or a timid, neurotic soul favored by God, but not a giant of strength and valor. What can explain the disparity between two biblical records, of David's inward and outward journeys?

We all experience both an inner life and an outer life simultaneously. We perceive life as a kind of movie, consisting of characters and sets and twists of plot—with ourselves playing the starring roles. If I attend the same event as you (say, a party), I will take home similar "outer" facts about what happened and who was there, but a wholly different "inner" point of view. My memory will dwell on what impression I made. Was I witty or charming? Did I offend someone, or embarrass myself? Did I look good to others? Most likely you will ask the same questions, but about yourself.

David, however, seemed to view life a little differently. His exploits—killing wild animals bare-handed, felling Goliath, surviving Saul's onslaughts, routing the Philistines—surely earned him a starring role. But as he reflected on those events, and wrote poems about them, he found a way to make Yahweh, God of Israel, the one on center stage. Whatever the phrase "practicing the presence of God" means, David experienced it. Whether he expressed that presence in lofty poems of praise, or in an earthy harangue, in either case he intentionally involved God in the details of his life.

David had confidence that he mattered to God. After one narrow escape he wrote, "[God] rescued me because he delighted in me" (Psalm 18:19). . . .

Throughout his life David believed, truly believed, that the invisible world of God, heaven, and the angels was every bit as real as his own world of swords and spears and caves and thrones. The psalms form a record of his conscious effort to subject his own daily life to the reality of that invisible world beyond him.

Psalm 57 illustrates this process as well as any. David composed it, the title says, when he had fled from Saul into a cave. First Samuel 24 sets the scene: Saul with his well-armed hordes had completely encircled David's small band. Blocked off from all escape, David holed up in a cave next to a sheep pen.

The psalm expresses anxiety and fear, of course. But it ends with an oddly triumphant imperative, "Be exalted, O God, above the heavens; let your glory be over all the earth." Somehow, in the process of writing, David was able to lift his eyes from the dank, smelly cave to the heavens above. In the most unlikely of settings, he came to affirm, simply, "God reigns."

Perhaps it was the next morning that David strode out, unarmed, and confronted King Saul's entire army with no weapon but an appeal to conscience. Perhaps the very process of writing the psalm had emboldened him for such a bravura display of moral courage.

Few of us, thankfully, live on the edge of mortal danger, as David did. But we do, like David, have times when nerves fail, when fear creeps in, when it seems that God has withdrawn, when hostile forces have us surrounded. At such a moment I turn to the Psalms. I have a sneaking suspicion that David wrote psalms as a form of spiritual therapy, a way of "talking himself into" faith when his spirit and emotions were wavering. And now, centuries later, we can use those very same prayers as steps of faith, a path to lead us from an obsession with ourselves to the actual presence of our God.

Your Fresh Take

Have you ever experienced a time when you were only able to "fight a giant" after you had privately (in a journal, in prayer, or in conversation with a confidant) laid out your worries, doubts, and fears? How or why might the process of naming obstacles and fear ultimately lead to the expression of faith or to acts of courage? _____

_____

_____

_____

As a form of "spiritual therapy," write a short psalm that puts God at center stage of your current life situation. End with praise or a claim of faith—as boldly as you are able. _____

_____

_____

_____

Read Psalms 56 and 57. Make David's psalms your own—allowing them to be windows that open you to the presence of God in your situation. _____

_____

_____

_____

Lord, as I Open . . .

MYSELF TO THE REAL-LIFE STRUGGLES—FEAR AND
FAITH—EXPRESSED BY DAVID THE PSALMIST, TEACH
ME HOW TO PUT YOU RATHER THAN MYSELF AT THE
CENTER OF MY "LIFE SCRIPT," TURNING TO YOU FOR
STRENGTH, GIVING YOU CREDIT FOR MY VICTORIES,
ASSURED OF YOUR PRESENCE. AMEN.

NOTHING CAN BE SO IRRITATING AS
A "THORN IN THE FLESH"
RELATIONSHIP WE
CANNOT AVOID WITH A
PERSON WE CANNOT STAND!

*Why do you look at the speck of sawdust
in your brother's eye and pay no
attention to the plank in your own eye?*

LUKE 6:41

CHAPTER 11

OPEN TO
LIFE-CHANGING PRAYER

Reflection
JOHN GUEST

More often than not we become the answer to our own prayers as we open up ourselves to God in prayer.

We so easily overlook this! We come to God in prayer detached from the very situation we are praying about, as though we had nothing to do with it. "God, change the situation," we pray, or "Lord, make this difficult relationship work better," or "Jesus, resolve this complicated problem." All the while we fail to take account of the obvious fact that we are part of the awkward situation, the difficult relationship, the complicated problem. If God actually is to change it, will He not begin by changing us and the part we have to play in it? The very fact we are concerned about the problem, and are bringing it before Him in prayer, makes us prime candidates to be used by Him in solving it! . . .

Nowhere is this principle more applicable than

in the area of personal relationships. Nothing can be so irritating as a "thorn in the flesh" relationship we cannot avoid with a person we cannot stand! It may be a neighbor or a coworker. It may be a boss. It may even—on a more temporary basis, one hopes—be husband or wife, parent or child. How many times have we come before the Lord, hot and hurt, frustrated and confused, and pleaded with Him: "Lord, isn't there anything You can do about this?"

But remember, it takes two. Any troubled relationship involves not only the other person—who so often becomes the exclusive focus of our prayer— but ourselves as well. Even though we may consider them the real problem, it is wonderful how, once we begin to pray, God changes us. Paul told the Romans, "If possible, so far as it depends upon you, live peaceably with all" (Romans 12:18 RSV). We are not entirely the cause of every relationship difficulty we experience—but we do have some part in it. Asking God to show us where we are at fault and to change us may not be where the process ends, but marvelously it is where it invariably begins.

. . . Don worked in a large insurance company. His boss in that company was a man he simply couldn't stand. It got to the point where the boss dominated Don's life because Don hated him so. All Don could think about was how miserable this man was making his life, and about what he was going to say or do the next time he saw him. It was eating him alive, giving him sleepless nights.

Finally, Don shared his situation with a friend, the Reverend Sam Shoemaker. "Don, you've got some serious praying to do," Sam told him. "You've got to start praying for this man you find so unbearable." . . . It went against his very nature, but Don finally accepted the challenge and put prayer into action. He gave it a try.

One day, a few months later, as Don was passing his boss's office, the man called him in.

"What is it with you?" the man said in a puzzled voice.

"What do you mean?" asked Don.

"I mean what's happened to you? You've changed!"

It turned out, as it so often does, that the relationship problem which was causing Don such grief owed as much to Don's attitude as to his boss. How it got started Don could never quite say. But before it could be resolved, a fundamental change had to take place in Don. When Don began to pray earnestly for his boss, it was his own heart that God changed. God's method for resolving the problem invariably is to change the one who prays.

Not all our problems are as extreme as Don's, nor will the answers to them always be so clear-cut and dramatic. But the basic principle is the same: God can change outside circumstances, and He frequently does. But more often than not He changes *us*.

YOUR FRESH TAKE

Consider a time when you have prayed for God to change someone else—only to be surprised that He changed *you*. _____
_____
_____
_____
_____

Think of one current situation (or relationship) you would like God to change. Can you even imagine anything God might change in you to bring this situation to a higher, healthier plane? _____
_____
_____
_____
_____

Why is it hard to retain resentment and bitterness toward someone you are praying for? _____
_____
_____
_____
_____

Lord, as I Open . . .

MYSELF TO YOU IN PRAYER, I PRAY FOR THE
PEOPLE WHO FEEL LIKE THORNS TO ME. I ASK
THAT YOU CHANGE THEM AND THE TENOR OF
OUR RELATIONSHIP. IF THIS MEANS YOU NEED
TO CHANGE ME, OKAY. I THINK I'M READY, AND
I TRUST MYSELF TO YOUR RENEWING WAYS. IN
JESUS'S NAME, AMEN.

A TEARDROP ON EARTH SUMMONS
THE KING OF HEAVEN.

You have kept count of my tossings;
put my tears in your bottle.
Are they not in your record?

PSALM 56:8 NRSV

CHAPTER 12

OPEN TO
EMOTION

Reflection
CHARLES R. SWINDOLL

When words fail, tears flow. Tears have a language all their own, a tongue that needs no interpreter. In some mysterious way our complex inner-communication system knows when to admit its verbal limitations . . . and the tears come.

Eyes that flashed and sparkled only moments before are flooded from a secret reservoir. We try in vain to restrain the flow, but even strong men falter.

Tears are not self-conscious. They can spring upon us when we are speaking in public, or standing beside others who look to us for strength. Most often they appear when our soul is overwhelmed with feelings that words cannot describe.

Our tears may flow during the singing of a great, majestic hymn, or when we are alone, lost in some vivid memory or wrestling in prayer.

Did you know that God takes special notice of

those tears of yours? Psalm 56:8 tells that He puts them in His bottle and enters them into the record He keeps on our lives.

David said, "The Lord hath heard the voice of my weeping" (Psalm 6:8 KJV).

A teardrop on earth summons the King of heaven. Rather than being ashamed or disappointed, the Lord takes note of our inner friction when hard times are oiled by tears. He turns these situations into moments of tenderness; He never forgets those crises in our lives where tears were shed.

One of the great drawbacks of our cold, sophisticated society is its reluctance to show tears. For some strange reason men feel that tears are a sign of weakness . . . and many an adult feels to cry is to be immature. How silly! How unfortunate! The consequence is that we place a watchdog named "restraint" before our hearts. This animal is trained to bark, snap, and scare away any unexpected guest who seeks entrance.

The ultimate result is a well-guarded, highly respectable, uninvolved heart surrounded by heavy bars of confinement. Such a structure resembles a prison more than a home where the tender Spirit of Christ resides.

Jeremiah lived in no such dwelling. His transparent tent was so tender and sensitive, he could not preach a sermon without the interruption of tears. "The weeping prophet" became his nickname, and even though he didn't always have the words to describe his feelings, he was never at a loss to communicate his convictions. You could always count on Jeremiah to bury his head in his hands and sob aloud.

Strange that this man was selected by God to be His personal spokesman at the most critical time in Israel's history. Seems like an unlikely choice—unless you value tears as God does. I wonder how many tear bottles in heaven are marked with his name.

I wonder how many of them bear *your* initials. You'll never have many until you impound restraint and let a little tenderness run loose. You might lose a little of your polished respectability, but you'll have a lot more freedom. And a lot less pride.

Your Fresh Take

Note John 11:35, which says that Jesus wept at circumstances surrounding the death of His friend Lazarus. Note also Mark 14:72, which says that Peter wept when he realized the gravity of his sin. Read all of Psalm 56—a description of David's tears. What is most likely to make you overflow with emotion?

_____

_____

Describe a specific time when you felt that opening yourself to tenderness brought some measure of freedom to your spirit. _____

_____

_____

_____

Think of your present situation. What issue might be starting to dam up emotion in you? As you open yourself to the Spirit of Christ, what do you sense Him asking you to do with your excess emotion?

_____

_____

_____

What do you want God to do with the tears you shed?

_____

_____

Lord, I Open . . .

MY HEART TO RECEIVING THE GIFT OF TEARS. THIS
FRIGHTENS ME A BIT. ACCEPT MY TEARS. HEAR
MY PRAYER. ALLOW ME TO KNOW THAT THOUGH
TEARS MAY LAST FOR A SEASON, YOUR PEACE AND
FREEDOM WILL FOLLOW. THROUGH YOUR SON I
PRAY, AMEN.

I JOURNALED ALL THE SCRIPTURES ABOUT GOD'S PRESENCE WITH AND WITHIN US, TURNING THEM INTO PETITIONARY PRAYERS.

Delight yourself in the LORD and he will give you the desires of your heart.

PSALM 37:4

CHAPTER 13

OPEN TO
PRAYER OF THE HEART

Reflection
LEANNE PAYNE

As we continue to lift up our longings before the Lord, we gain understanding of our own hearts. We also grow in the knowledge of how best to pray for ourselves, others, and the situations surrounding us. At times, therefore, we modify or even strike through a petition and replace it with something better. In this activity we grow in wisdom, understanding, and knowledge as we gain the will of God. We even gain the mind of Christ in regard to our petitions.

Prayer is powerful. We can release our faith amiss, or in the wrong timing. Christ has said: "Ask and it will be given to you; seek and you will find; knock and the door will be opened to you. For everyone who asks receives; he who seeks finds; and to him who knocks, the door will be opened" (Matthew 7:7–8).

It is important, therefore, to ask always for God's mind and even His most perfect will on our petitions.

To persevere with God in this way is a needful thing. We ask, we seek, we continue to knock, and like the persistent widow of Luke 18:5, we receive. . . .

Until we learn to yield to God all the needs, cries, and desires of our hearts in petition, we will know neither Him nor our hearts as we should. To come present to Him and to our hearts is to cry out our personal petitions. Then we must have ears to hear His heart for us: His desires, promises, exhortations, and commands. In this way we no longer pray merely by rote but achieve the "prayer of the heart."

I will never forget the joy of first coming into this prayer of the heart. I had much need and therefore much to lay out before Him. As I was finding and holding close to my heart His promises, my petitions began to multiply. After all, does it not say in James: "You do not have, because you do not ask God" (4:2)? From early on, this section in my [prayer] journal has been a large one.

I learned to head my petitionary lists with scriptures that urged me on to greater faith, such as, "Until now you have not asked for anything in my name. Ask and you will receive, and your joy will be complete" (John 16:24) and "If you believe, you will receive whatever you ask for in prayer" (Matthew 21:22). It is wonderful to go back through my journals and recount God's answers to prayer. Sometimes when something remarkable has happened, I find in reviewing some old prayer journal where I specifically petitioned the Lord for this thing. "No wonder this marvelous thing has happened!" I find myself exclaiming aloud. There is nothing surer on this earth than the truth that God hears and answers prayer. It has been said that it is a rule of the Father's house that we *ask* for what we get. The Scriptures certainly admonish us to ask. Then we need only learn to *receive* of the abundance He sends.

In those first days of learning to lay my heart before God—which is what the prayer of petition enabled me to do—I received more healing and understanding than one could well imagine. The Psalms, with their wonderful promises, provided a bounteous and boundless seedbed of petitions in my early journaling. "Delight yourself in the LORD and he will give you the desires of your heart" (37:4) especially exercised me. Just how does one delight oneself in the Lord, I asked over and over. What were the desires of my heart? I did not know. They were too repressed; I had little hope for them. I searched the Scriptures for clues, and those that proclaim God's presence with us stood out. King David had the answer: "In thy presence is fulness of joy" (Psalm 16:11 KJV).

. . . I journaled all the Scriptures about God's presence with and within us, turning them into petitionary prayers. I meditated on them, asked questions of the Lord about them, listened to hear what He would speak to me about them—and was led straight into the practice of the presence!

YOUR FRESH TAKE

Think back over your recent petitions to God. What do your requests tell you about the desires of your heart? For the next week keep a daily prayer journal that includes a list of your petitions. _____

_____

_____

_____

_____

As you have matured in your faith and knowledge of God, how have your prayer-petitions changed? Do you sense that your heart is more closely aligned with God's heart than it was five years ago? How or why?

_____

_____

_____

_____

Choose several Scripture passages that are meaningful to you. Turn them into petitionary prayers. To edify other Christians, discuss how God has made His presence real to you as you have turned biblical promises into petitions and waited in faith for God to work.

_____

_____

_____

_____

Lord, I Open . . .

MY HEART TO YOU, PRESENTING MY NEEDS AND
DESIRES BEFORE YOU AS PETITIONS. THIS MAKES ME
FEEL VULNERABLE, BECAUSE AS I SHOW YOU MY NAKED
HEART, I SEE IT MYSELF. PLEASE BE TENDER WITH ME
AS YOU DRAW ME CLOSER INTO YOUR PRESENCE
AND MOLD MY HEART TO THE LIKENESS OF YOURS.
THROUGH YOUR SON I COME, AMEN.

I THINK THAT GOD REQUIRED
THE ISRAELITES TO GATHER
MANNA EVERY MORNING SO
THAT THEY WOULD LEARN
TO COME TO HIM DAILY.

I have treasured the words of his mouth
more than my daily bread.

JOB 23:12

CHAPTER 14

OPEN TO THE HEART OF GOD

Reflection
CYNTHIA HEALD

I can't believe that all we get to eat is this manna—
the same thing every day! And each morning we have
to gather it all over again. Why can't we just collect a
few days' worth, a couple of times a week? The other
day I got a little more than I needed, and boy, did it
ever spoil. My stomach still turns at the thought of
how those worms looked. Okay, sure, it's nourishing,
and although it's nothing to write home about, I'll
admit it's satisfying. But morning after morning after
morning, we're up doing the same thing. I guess we
have to if we want to stay alive and have strength to
travel."

It is necessary to eat every day to maintain strength
and energy. When we don't, our bodies weaken. The
same is true with our spirits. To maintain spiritual
strength, we must feed our spirits every day with the
Word of God, our spiritual food. I think that God

required the Israelites to gather manna every morning so that they would learn to come to Him daily.

I once heard someone observe that spiritual eating operates in the opposite way from physical eating. If we don't eat physically, we grow hungry. Once we consume food, the hunger subsides and we feel satisfied. If we don't eat spiritually, we can lose our spiritual appetite. The less we eat spiritually, the less hungry we become. But the more we are nourished by the Word of God, the hungrier we become for spiritual food.

In another sense, however, the two forms of intake are alike. If you stop eating physically, you can count on family, friends, and medical professionals to urge or even coerce you into getting some food into you before you grow dangerously weak. They will know that the weaker you get, the less you may feel the desire to eat. I think this is true in the spiritual realm also. When you don't *feel* like reading the Scriptures (you're not getting anything out of it; you don't have the time; you're just not up for it), that is the very time you need to be sure to stay strong spiritually. Jesus's rebuke of Satan, while He was physically weak from fasting, illustrates this very point. Tempted to turn rocks into bread, the Lord responded by quoting the Scriptures, which gave Him spiritual strength to resist the devil's attack: "No! The Scriptures say, 'People need more than bread for their life; they must feed on every word of God'" (Matthew 4:4 NLT).

The Bible is *the* guidebook to the heart of God. It tells us everything we need to know about how to make this journey. It gives direction; it teaches; it corrects; it trains. It is God's Holy Spirit-breathed book for us to read, study, and meditate on. Through consistent intake of this, we will grow strong. Here we will find the revelation of our heavenly Father's character. Here we will discover His love for His people. . . .

I read the Word of God, I study it, I memorize it, and I meditate on it because I love it, and because I want to grow and learn and be changed into His image. I do not consider this a spiritual discipline in the sense that it is something that *should* and *ought to* be done. I spend time with the Lord and His Word because doing so is the joy and delight of my heart. His Word is ever new, and His Spirit continually teaches and transforms me. Why would anything this world offers or demands keep me from the eternal richness and blessing of being with, and listening to, my Lord? This Guidebook is the ultimate guidebook, and it leads me straight to the heart of God.

YOUR FRESH TAKE

Think of a time when you were keenly aware that yesterday's physical nutrition was not going to sustain you today. What happened when you "ran out of steam" and when you got new sustenance? How is spiritual sustenance like and unlike physical sustenance?

_____

_____

_____

You may have gone through seasons when Bible reading was difficult for you. What makes it hard for you to open the Book? (Think in practical terms—schedules, lack of a quiet place—and also in spiritual terms.) What specific changes can you make to eliminate these obstacles?_____

_____

_____

_____

Read 2 Timothy 3:14–17. Rephrase these verses in your own words, as a prayer of thanksgiving for the role of Scripture in your life. Then pray for continued strength from the Scripture as you face today and look toward tomorrow._____

_____

_____

_____

Lord, as I Open . . .

MY BIBLE TO "EAT" AND INWARDLY DIGEST YOUR
WORD, SUSTAIN MY FAITH AND MY ENERGY AS I SET
OUT TO ADDRESS EVERY GOOD WORK YOU HAVE
FOR ME TO DO. SPEAK, LORD, FOR YOUR SERVANT
WANTS TO HEAR YOUR HEART. FEED ME WITH
THE BREAD OF LIFE. KEEP ME HUNGRY FOR YOU.
IN JESUS'S NAME, AMEN.

IT IS THE ONLY SPIRITUAL DISCIPLINE

I HAVE EVER REALLY STUCK WITH,

AND I AM NOT TEMPTED TO

ABANDON IT, BECAUSE IT HAS MADE

MY LIFE SO MUCH RICHER.

When he, the Spirit of truth, comes,
he will guide you into all truth.

JOHN 16:13

CHAPTER 15

OPEN TO THE
SPIRIT'S LEADING

Reflection
BILL HYBELS

As believers, of course, we are responsible to obey God's entire Word. But the Bible is a big book, and we can't swallow it all at once. So God often gives us His truth a bite-sized piece at a time. This is what He did for me.

When I became a Christian at age sixteen, I felt the Holy Spirit saying to me, "You need to understand doctrine: the difference between grace and good works as a means of getting to heaven, the meaning of faith, the identity of God, the person of Jesus Christ, the work of the Holy Spirit." So I studied and prayed and talked to friends and took courses on doctrinal issues.

A few years later the focus changed. Now the emphasis was on character. Every time I turned around the Holy Spirit seemed to say to me, "You need to grow in sensitivity and compassion." I have a hard time being a kind, gentle, tenderhearted person; my personality is not naturally that way. And so I read and studied and memorized verses like Ephesians 4:32: "Be kind and compassionate to one another, forgiving each other, just as in Christ God forgave you."

Later, after I married, the Holy Spirit pierced my soul as if with daggers and said, "You are not living like a godly husband; you do not treasure your wife 'as Christ loved the church and gave himself up for her'" (Ephesians 5:25). Right now the most important thing for you to learn is how to be a loving husband."

In recent years the Holy Spirit has urged me to study prayer—how we can best communicate with God, and how He speaks to us. Next month, next year, He will probably lead me to focus on a different truth.

If you remain sensitive to the Holy Spirit's leadings and cooperate with them, you can trust Him to guide you into the truth and to help you grow up as a Christian. That doesn't give you license to ignore parts of Scripture and say, "Well, that's not what the Holy Spirit is emphasizing in my life right now." We're responsible for the whole Word of God. Nevertheless, the Holy Spirit has a way of emphasizing different areas at different times. . . .

God's power is available to us when we come to Him in solitude, when we learn how to focus and center our hearts and be quiet before Him. When we learn the discipline of stillness before God, we find that His leadings come through to us clearly, with little interference.

That is why I have made the commitment to spend from half an hour to an hour every single morning in a secluded place with the Lord. I don't do this to earn merit badges from God. I expect no brownie points for my devotional patterns. I do it because I grew very tired of leading an unexamined life.

I used to try to pray and receive God's leadings on the run. It became obvious to me that the pace of my life outstripped my capacity to analyze it. It exhausted me to be constantly doing and rarely reflecting on what I did. At the end of a day, I would wonder if my work had any meaning at all.

So I developed my own disciplined approach to stillness before God. It is the only spiritual discipline I have ever really stuck with, and I am not tempted to abandon it, because it has made my life so much richer.

. . . First I write a page in my journal. Starting with the word *yesterday*, I chronicle God's activity in my life the previous day. Then I write out my prayers, using the categories of adoration, confession, thanksgiving, and supplication.

When I have done that, my spirit is quiet and receptive. That is when I write an *L* for *listen* on a piece of paper and circle it. Then I sit quietly and simply say, "Now, Lord, I invite You to speak to me by Your Holy Spirit."

The moments with God that follow are the ones that really matter.

YOUR FRESH TAKE

Name two or three potential benefits of spending half an hour each day being still before God in prayer. (If you already practice this disciplined pattern, think of real benefits, considering your life situation.) _____

_____

_____

_____

_____

As you currently read the Word of God and listen to His Spirit, what truth or Christian principle does God's spotlight seem to illuminate? What was the spotlighted "lesson" for you five years ago? Can you see a pattern of growth in light of the "entire Word"?

_____

_____

_____

_____

Reflect on God's presence and work in your life yesterday. What meaning do you see in your work, your conversations, and your activities? Then write a four-sentence prayer that includes adoration, confession, thanksgiving, and supplication. _____

_____

_____

_____

_____

Lord, as I Open . . .

MY LIFE AND HEART TO YOU AND YOUR PURPOSES,
GIVE ME THE DESIRE TO SPEND TIME LISTENING TO
THE STILL, SMALL VOICE OF YOUR SPIRIT AS I REFLECT
ON MY WALK WITH YOU AND YOUR WORK IN MY LIFE.
TO YOUR GLORY. THROUGH CHRIST, AMEN.

We cannot experience the fullness of Christ if we do all the expressing. We must also allow God to express His love, will, and truth to us.

*Your word is a lamp to my feet
and a light for my path. . . .
I have put my hope in your word.*

PSALM 119:105, 114

CHAPTER 16

OPEN TO GOD'S COMMUNICATION

Reflection
GARY SMALLEY

Prayer is two-way communication. Just as true friendship requires equal participation from each member, so does our relationship with God. We cannot experience the fullness of Christ if we do all the expressing. We must also allow God to express His love, will, and truth to us. (He promised to teach us His knowledge through His Spirit [see Proverbs 1].) We can listen to Him in many ways, but the three I use most often are reading the Word, picturing it, and waiting for His peace. . . .

Picturing God's Word in our minds, the second aspect of listening to God, familiarizes us with a verse, a passage, a chapter, even an entire book in the Bible. It is especially helpful when we don't have access to a Bible.

I try to picture God's Word when I'm running or have some idle time. One morning I read the story of how Jesus healed the woman who touched the hem of His garment. Later that day I imagined being at the scene, bringing it to life on my mental screen. I felt and smelled the people pressing around us. I heard the beggars shouting. I saw the lame pushing and shoving, trying to get through. I heard Christ ask who touched Him, and I watched the woman tremble as she came forward. I heard Him speak to her: "Daughter, your faith has made you well; go in peace, and be healed of your affliction" (see Mark 5:34). Like the disciples, I wondered how Jesus felt one woman's touch among such a crowd. I glimpsed His sensitivity—He cared for someone I and the others had ignored. I saw faith and love firsthand. . . .

Another way to listen to God is to wait for His peace. One of the streets on which I jog passes a new development where each lot has a beautiful, panoramic view of Phoenix. A few years ago one lot caught my attention. It was expensive, but I figured I could save for it.

Norma and I got in line, praying that God would allow us to purchase the lot so we could build our dream home. Although we never had complete peace about it, I continued to pray. Finally, when we had saved enough money, I checked with the owner and learned that the lot had tripled in price. This forced us to reevaluate God's will in our lives. We determined that His will for us at that time was to use our income in ministry, not in a new home. With that settled, we were free and at peace to stay where we were.

The peace of God should rule in our hearts (Philippians 4:7). One meaning of the Greek word translated *rule* is *to be the umpire*.

Peace, or lack of it, is one way God has of telling us whether we are out or safe, and whether a situation is fair or foul. This does not mean we can never make a decision until we feel some kind of mystical peace. Some people, by their very nature, would never make any decision if they had to wait until they felt peace about it. It means instead that we can be at peace about doing the things God's Word specifically says we should do. For instance, God says we should go to a brother or sister we've offended and ask forgiveness. Therefore, we can have peace about doing it, even though we feel anything but peaceful on the way over to do it.

As we experience God's peace, hear Him speak to us through Scripture, and see His answers to prayer, we will be motivated to worship and praise Him even more.

YOUR FRESH TAKE

Choose one gospel story, and imagine that you are a character in it—that Jesus is talking to you or talking about you (as in a parable). Listen and allow the Holy Spirit to talk to your spirit. Discuss or write in a journal any new insight._____
_____
_____
_____

Read Philippians 4:7: "And the peace of God, which transcends all understanding, will guard your hearts and your minds in Christ Jesus." Have you ever experienced a time when inner peace and scriptural guidelines were indeed an "umpire" in your life, indicating what direction would be "fair" rather than "foul"? What was the outcome? _____
_____
_____
_____

Consider also Colossians 3:15: "Let the peace of Christ rule in your hearts, since as members of one body you were called to peace. And be thankful." How does your internal peace influence peace in your relationships with others?_____
_____
_____
_____

Lord, as I Open . . .

MYSELF TO YOU, I ASK FOR THE GRACE OF YOUR PEACE
IN MY SPIRIT. EVEN IN THE MIDST OF A TURBULENT
WORLD, I KNOW YOU ARE ABLE TO KEEP ME CALM.
SHOW ME THE PATH TO PEACE. I WANT TO WALK ON
THAT ROAD. THROUGH CHRIST, AMEN.

PART 3

WINDOWS OF
WONDER

Every now and then,
big, dark, round eyes
glanced at him
and then in the direction of
the portrait. She knew
he knew something
he wasn't telling her.

*I stand at the door and knock. If anyone hears
my voice and opens the door, I will come in.*

Revelation 3:20

CHAPTER 17

OPEN TO THE
TUG OF A CHILD

Reflection
JIM McGUIGGAN

It was July 11, 1971—a very good year. In Northern Ireland that week of July means flute bands; processions of marchers thousands strong; Union Jack flags; curbstones painted red, white, and blue; streets decorated with mock city walls, streamers, and wall paintings; dancing in the streets; and bonfires at every other intersection. And there was booze—yes, plenty of booze—and pubs packed to the doors. This was the time when the Protestant/Unionists celebrate an ancient victory over the Nationalist/Catholic forces.

One of the thousands of marchers in the Orange Order was Johnny Martin, who each year carried the symbolic saber as he marched triumphantly to the field where the multitude, weary with the march, would be glad to sit and listen to a series of speakers calling them to maintain the Union (with Britain).

Johnny was a painter by trade and a hard drinker by habit . . . .

When [his daughter] Ethel and her daughter, Linda, went to see the bonfire one 11th of July, Johnny had already been drunk and sober several times that day. Up the street he came, well into another binge, extra whiskey in his pockets and plenty of time to get it down. He tried to cuddle his six-year-old granddaughter, Linda, but she began to cry big tears and to tell him she didn't like the way he smelled. That broke his heart, and then and there he swore to her that he would never drink again. That very night he gave his life to Christ, the booze was dumped, and Johnny Martin hasn't had a drop in over twenty years.

Marvelous! This kind of turnaround is by no means rare, but it's remarkable just the same.

It's funny how many things God uses in His attempts to turn us around. . . .

A story is told of a man who took his little girl to an art gallery. She showed no interest at all until they came to a picture of a tired looking man, knocking and knocking on a door. The picture showed people on the other side of the door—it looked as if they had no plans to open it. She was hooked.

"Who is that?" she asked her dad. How could she know the question would trouble his heart—a heart that was wrestling with deep questions.

"It's Jesus," he heard himself say with a slight edge to his voice.

A pause, and then: "Won't they let Him in?"

Unease began to grow in the man, but he could hardly brush her off, so he quietly said: "No, they won't let Him in."

Quick as light, she asked: "Is He bad?"

And he shot back just as fast: "No! He isn't bad."

Faster still, she demanded: "Well, then, why won't they let Him in?"

Now he was really uneasy. He'd had enough, and as he gently but firmly walked her away from the picture, he heard himself say in a tone too terse: "How do I know?" She sensed the tension and said no more, but every now and then big, dark, round eyes glanced at him and then in the direction of the portrait. She knew he knew something he wasn't telling her.

At supper no word was said about it, but the eyes kept talking. After supper she got ready for bed, and with pajamas on and with toothpaste still around her mouth, she climbed up on his lap and hugged his neck longer than usual. Then she kissed him, headed for the bedroom, stopped, turned, and said: "We'd let Him in, wouldn't we?"

Then off she went to sleep like a rock, while all through a grown man's sleepless night, God pried his heart open with a child's words.

I'm told that just like my father-in-law, Johnny Martin, the man "let Him in."

YOUR FRESH TAKE

Consider Luke 18:17: "Anyone who will not receive the kingdom of God like a little child will never enter it." Think about the children you have known (maybe even a childhood playmate or yourself as a child). What childlike qualities draw them—and us adults—near to the heart of God? _____

_____

_____

_____

_____

Name one childlike quality that is still strong in your spirit or personality. Name one childlike quality you would like to revive._____

_____

_____

_____

Think of the various rooms in a typical house. Imagine comparable rooms in your heart. Imagine Jesus knocking at the door of one of your heart-rooms that you have barred shut. What door is He knocking at? Can you open it? Why or why not?_____

_____

_____

_____

Lord, as I Open . . .

A CLOSED DOOR OF MY HEART TO YOU, I ASK THAT
YOU INCREASE THE CHILDLIKE FAITH AND TRUST
THAT IS KEY TO LIFE IN YOUR KINGDOM. KEEP THE
CHILD IN ME ATTUNED TO THE CHILDREN IN MY LIFE.
USE THEIR INNOCENT WORDS AND WONDER TO TUG
ME TOWARD YOU. THROUGH JESUS THE SON, AMEN.

DO YOU UNDERSTAND WHAT
IS GOING ON IN THE
INVISIBLE REALM OF YOUR
LIFE WITH GOD?

*You hem me in—behind and before; you have
laid your hand upon me. Such knowledge is too
wonderful for me, too lofty for me to attain.*

PSALM 139:5–6

CHAPTER 18

OPEN TO THE MYSTERY

Reflection
ELISABETH ELLIOT

Some things are simply too wonderful for explanation—the navigational system of the Arctic tern, for example. How does it find its way over twelve thousand miles of ocean from its nesting grounds in the Arctic to its wintering grounds in the Antarctic! Ornithologists have conducted all sorts of tests without finding the answer. Instinct is the best they can offer—no explanation at all, merely a way of saying that they really have no idea. . . .

When the angel Gabriel told Mary, "You will be with child and give birth to a son," she had a simple question about the natural: How can this be, since I am a virgin?!

The answer had to do not with the natural but with something far more mysterious than the tern's navigation—something, in fact, entirely supernatural: "The Holy Spirit will come upon you, and the power of the Most High will overshadow you" (Luke 1:35). That was too wonderful, and Mary was silent. She had no question about the supernatural. She was satisfied with God's answer.

The truth about the Incarnation is a thing too wonderful for us. Who can fathom what really took place first in a virgin's womb in Nazareth and then in a stable in Bethlehem!

At the end of the book of Job, instead of answering his questions, God revealed to Job the mystery of who He was. Then Job despised himself. "I have uttered what I did not understand, / things too wonderful for me, which I did not know" (Job 42:3 RSV).

In one of David's "songs of ascents," he wrote, "My heart is not proud, O LORD, / my eyes are not haughty; / I do not concern myself with great matters / or things too wonderful for me. / But I have stilled and quieted my soul" (Psalm 131:1–2).

A close and fretful inquiry into how spiritual things "work" is an exercise in futility. Even wondering how "natural" things are going to work if you bring God into them—how God will answer a prayer for money, for example . . . is sometimes an awful waste of energy. God knows how. Why should I bother my head about it if I've turned it over to Him? If the Word of the Lord to us is that we are "predestined according to the plan of him who works out everything in conformity with the purpose of his will" (Ephesians 1:11), we may apprehend this fact by faith alone. By believing that God means just what He says, and by acting upon the Word (faith always requires action), we apprehend it—we take hold of it, we make it our own. We cannot make it our own by mere reason—"I don't see how such-and-such an incident can possibly have anything to do with any divine 'plan.' "

Why should we *see* how! Is it not sufficient that we are told that it is so? We need not see. We need only believe and proceed on the basis of that assured fact. . . .

Do you understand what is going on in the invisible realm of your life with God? Do you *see* how the visible things relate to the hidden plan and purpose? Probably not. As my second husband Addison Leitch used to say, "You can't unscrew the Inscrutable." But you do see at least one thing, maybe a very little thing, that He wants you to do. "Now what I am commanding you today is not too difficult [other translations say too hard, too wonderful] for you or beyond your reach. It is not up in heaven . . . nor is it beyond the sea. . . . No, the word is very near you; it is in your mouth and in your heart so you may obey it" (Deuteronomy 30:11–14).

Let it suffice you, as it sufficed Mary, to know that God knows. If it's time to work, get on with your job. If it's time to go to bed, go to sleep in peace. Let the Lord of the Universe do the worrying.

Your Fresh Take

Name one specific characteristic of God that is "too wonderful" for you to grasp. Also name one aspect of God's creation that is beyond your comprehension and one aspect of God's work in your life that is "too wonderful." _____

_____

_____

_____

Think of a time when "a close and fretful inquiry" into spiritual workings kept you closed in, away from the "open window" of spiritual freshness. _____

_____

_____

_____

In light of your responses to these suggested activities, consider God's Word in Deuteronomy 30:11–14: "Now what I am commanding you today is not too difficult [too wonderful] for you or beyond your reach. It is not up in heaven . . . nor is it beyond the sea. . . . No, the word is very near you; it is in your mouth and in your heart so you may obey it." What focus does this give you as you plan your week?

_____

_____

_____

Lord, as I Open . . .

MYSELF TO UNDERSTANDING THAT YOU AND YOUR WAYS ARE BEYOND MY UNDERSTANDING, CALM MY FRETFUL WORRIES. LET ME REST IN YOUR INSCRUTABLE BUT VERY REAL PRESENCE IN MY LIFE AND WORLD. THROUGH JESUS, AMEN.

IT WAS AS THOUGH MY EYES
HAD BEEN OPENED AND
I SAW A NEW PERSON.

*Is not the bread that we break a
participation in the body of Christ?*

1 CORINTHIANS 10:16

CHAPTER 19

OPEN TO THE BROKEN BODY

Reflection
PAUL BRAND

The caste system in India is pervasive. . . .

The lowest stratum of society is the deformed leprosy patient. Doctors, lawyers, and priests are looked upon as the highest stratum, and are treated with great deference. I have often been embarrassed by the way patients will bow to the ground and touch my feet before I have a chance to stop them.

In our leprosy sanitarium at Karigiri in South India we have a lovely chapel, made from stones that have been hewn from the surrounding rocky hills. In that chapel during the season of Lent, we have an early morning communion service every Wednesday. It is open to Christian staff and patients, and is led by one of the doctors who is also an ordained presbyter of the Church of South India. The numbers are few at that early hour, and we stand in a circle around the table, passing the bread and the wine from hand to hand. In turn, we speak the name of the person to our left, and use the scriptural words that define the elements that we share.

On the day I remember best, the person to my right was a leprosy patient, Manikam, a beggar on whose deformed hands I had operated a few weeks before. He had come to know the Lord, and was happy both in the improvement in his hands as well as in his new faith. In the hospital ward, however, it was still difficult to get him look at the doctors, as he responded to our questions. His downcast eyes still identified him as an outcast.

As the plate with the bread came around the circle, Manikam took his piece, and then took the plate to pass it to me. Because his hands were still stiff from the recent surgery and plaster cast, as well as from the effect of his previous disease and injuries, he fumbled and almost dropped the plate. I reached out to steady it from him. Then he turned to me and held out the bread. His back was straight, his voice was clear and strong, and his eyes looked directly into mine. "Paul," he said, "this is the body of Christ, broken for you." As I took the bread, my eyes misted over, and I could hardly control my voice as I turned to pass the bread to the person on my left.

I cannot describe the delight I felt as I looked into Manikam's face and recognized the life of Jesus as he spoke the words, "The body of Christ, broken for you." It was as though my eyes had been opened and

I saw a new person. Jesus had broken hands, Jesus knew pain and rejection, and it was Jesus whose life and death had brought about the sense of love and fellowship that I experienced with my patient at that time. We were one loaf, one body, and shared one Lord.

This was a miracle. Anywhere but in that situation, and anytime in the past, he would have called me "Doctor Brand" and in a humble voice, with downcast eyes. To hear my name, Paul, ring out in the chapel, with the freedom and confidence of an equal member of the same body, was a most moving thing. All of us must have felt the transformation. We thanked God for the reality behind the symbol of the broken bread, broken from the one loaf. . . .

When I take the bread, I try to be thankful for three aspects of that broken bread that have significance for me. First, I remember the sacrifice of Jesus on the cross, when His body was broken for me. Then I think of the way in which His life continues to sustain me today; His body, the Living Bread.

Then I look around me and recognize those who are worshiping with me. I need to remind myself of our essential oneness, and I do it individually. Deliberately downplaying our differences, I seek to see Jesus in each one of them. That way it becomes, indeed, a love feast as well as a memorial service and, not least, a celebration of the continuing life of the Lord within me.

YOUR FRESH TAKE

Read Galatians 3:28–4:7. The first-century categories—Jew or Greek, slave or free—might now be represented by other categories. Personalize this passage so it is relevant to the "categories" of people in your own church and wider world. _____

_____

_____

_____

_____

Describe a time when, while taking communion, your eyes were opened to some spiritual insight about God, about yourself, or about other worshipers.

_____

_____

_____

_____

How does Paul Brand's insight of the body of Christ—broken on the cross, as represented in communion, or as represented in other believers—change your spiritual outlook, your view of fellowship, or your worship?_____

_____

_____

_____

_____

Lord, as I Open . . .

MYSELF TO YOU AND RECEIVE THE BROKEN BREAD REPRESENTING YOUR BROKEN BODY, OPEN MY SPIRITUAL EYES TO THE UNDERSTANDING OF YOUR SACRIFICE AND TO THE MEANING OF YOUR CHURCH BEING ONE UNIFIED BODY IN YOU, OUR LORD. IN JESUS'S NAME, AMEN.

EVERYWHERE WE LOOK, THERE ARE
PICTURES THAT ARE NOT
REALLY PICTURES BUT WINDOWS.

"LORD, open the eyes of these men so they can see."
Then the LORD opened their eyes and they looked.

2 KINGS 6:20

CHAPTER 20

OPEN TO THE "SECOND LOOK"

Reflection
KEN GIRE

We reach for God in many ways. Through our sculptures and our scriptures. Through our pictures and our prayers. Through our writing and our worship. And through them He reaches for us.

His search begins with something said. Ours begins with something heard. His begins with something shown. Ours, with something seen. Our search for God and His search for us meet at windows in our everyday experience.

These are the windows of the soul.

In a sense, it is something like spiritual disciplines for the spiritually undisciplined. In another sense, it is the most rigorous of disciplines—the discipline of awareness. For we must always be looking and listening if we are to see the windows and hear what is being spoken to us through them.

But we must learn to look with more than just our

eyes and listen with more than just our ears, for the sounds are sometimes faint and the sights sometimes far away. We must be aware, at all times and in all places, because windows are everywhere, and at any time we may find one.

Or one may find us. . . .

When we look long enough at a scene from a movie, a page from a book, a person from across the room, and when we look deeply enough, those moments framed in our minds grow transparent. Everywhere we look, there are pictures that are not really pictures but windows. If only we have eyes to see beyond the paint. If we look closely, we can see something beyond the two dimensions within the frame, something beyond the ordinary colors brushed across the canvas of our everyday lives.

What do we see in those windows? What do we see of who we are, or once were, or one day might become? What do we see of our neighbor living down the street or our neighbor living *on* the street? What do we see about God?

Windows of the soul is a way of seeing that begins with respect. The way we show respect is to give it a second look, a look not of the eyes but of the heart. But so often we don't give something a second look, because we don't think there is anything there to see.

To respect something is to understand that there is something there to see, that it is not all surface, that something lies beneath the surface, something that has the power to change the way we think or feel, something that may prove so profound a revelation as to change not only how we look at our lives but how we live them.

Jesus lived His life that way, seeing beyond the pictures of the widow at Nain and the woman at the well, of the tax collector in the tree and the thief on the cross, of the rich man and Lazarus.

He was constantly looking beyond the two dimensions of the full-sized portraits framed before Him. Beyond the widow's tears for her dead son, Jesus saw how much she needed that son to fill the hole left by her deceased husband. Beyond the Samaritan woman's veil, He saw the five marriages that had failed, and beyond that, the emptiness in her life that grew bigger with each divorce. Beyond the power and wealth of Zacchaeus, He saw a small man with a big hole in his heart that all the power and wealth in the world couldn't fill. Beyond the sores of Lazarus, He saw a soul of eternal worth. Beyond the clothes of the rich man, He saw a soul in rags.

Seeing windows of the soul was the way Jesus lived His life and the way He taught His disciples to live theirs.

YOUR FRESH TAKE

What do you think Ken Gire meant when he said there is "a way of seeing that begins with respect"?

_____

_____

_____

_____

Do you think it is easier to see "beyond the power and wealth" of an influential person or "beyond the sores" of a hurting person? Why? _____

_____

_____

_____

_____

Reflect on a time when an ordinary event became "transparent"—when you saw beyond the obvious to the spiritual reality, beyond the "frame" to the "window." _____

_____

_____

_____

_____

Lord, as I Open . . .

MY EYES TO THE VIEW BEYOND THE OBVIOUS, OPEN
MY WORLD TO THE DELIGHTS OF YOUR OUT-OF-
THIS-WORLD KINGDOM. THROUGH CHRIST, AMEN.

HOW ODD THAT GOD HUMBLES
HIMSELF TO BE SEEN IN THE
MOST ORDINARY BEAUTIES, THE
EVERYDAY, TAKEN-FOR-GRANTED
STUFF OF CREATION!

*Since the creation of the world God's invisible
qualities—his eternal power and divine
nature—have been clearly seen, being
understood from what has been made.*

ROMANS 1:20

CHAPTER 21

OPEN TO THE
"MIRROR OF LIFE"

Reflection
LUCI SHAW

In fall California farmers celebrate with pumpkin festivals; the fields and foothills blaze orange with pumpkins, and the closer you approach them, the larger they loom, plump and rounded and colorful as fall foliage. Halloween is approaching, and on the weekends thousands of vans and station wagons loaded with young families make their pilgrimage to the pumpkin fields. There's an annual contest for the largest pumpkin, and monsters of hundreds of pounds of misshapen squash flesh are weighed and celebrated. After Halloween the same fields are still spotted with this fruit of the vine, but now only the rejects are left—the ones no one chose, that were flat on one side or scarred or just plain too ugly even for a jack-o'-lantern. All that growth, all summer long, for nothing? All that plump, sturdy pumpkin flesh simply waiting to go to rot?

In the hot noon sun of a summer day, I once went with two of my daughters, Robin and Kristin, and my granddaughter, Lindsay, to a "u-pick" raspberry farm, where acres of bushes grow in green rows, from which you can pick your own berries and save some pennies. There we plucked, for eating and for making jam, twelve pounds of raspberries—huge hybrids, sweet, red-velvet pendants ripe enough to drop into our hands and thence into the plastic buckets slung around our necks.

As we slowly passed between the tall green thickets of bushes, starting and stopping, our fingers stained, our mouths tart with the taste of summer, we would be sure we had thoroughly stripped a certain bush. Then, as we crouched lower, we could see from a new angle all the hidden treasures that remained—berries hanging like red hearts, hiding behind the leaves, waiting for our nimble fingers.

I felt sad for the ones that never got picked (no one took the trouble to go slowly enough or search for them carefully enough), for the ones that seemed too small or too hard to reach. All that slow ripening, as the rains fell and the short, cool days turned long and warm—for nothing—fruit without fruitfulness.

Unpicked raspberries are like the ideas we never discover because we are too hurried, because we see or think superficially. Discarded pumpkins are like the precious people we ignore. They are like the images of the holy hinted at in creation. They are like the glimpses of God we miss because our eyes are half-closed or our attention distracted. Harvesting ideas, loving ordinary people, seeing correspondences between the seen and unseen worlds, and gleaning glimpses of God—such tasks, the same as berry picking, take time, thoroughness, concentration, and the willingness to crouch in the sandy soil, to peer upwards, to lift aside the raspberry leaves, to see deep into the heart of each bush, to penetrate its leafy green reality and value what we find there.

How odd that God humbles Himself to be seen in the most ordinary beauties, the everyday, taken-for-granted stuff of creation! Yet His image is stamped wherever we turn our eyes. The clues to divine reality are under our feet, they brush our hands, they rustle in our ears, they mark our bare legs with their sharpness, and they burn our retinas with their color.

Thomas à Kempis, in *The Imitation of Christ*, reassures us, "If your heart is straight with God, then every creature will be to you a mirror of life and a book of holy doctrine." We are faced so often with things we know but still need to learn. How marvelous it is that realities as mundane as sunlight, field lilies, apple trees, ripe berries, pumpkins, and the delighted cries of young children are lenses through which we may see God.

Your Fresh Take

Think of your childhood, particularly one moment of wonder, when in a muddy creek or a snowbank or a science class you discovered something amazing about God's creation. Try to capture and relive that "wow." Remember the childhood moment and why the memory is important to you. _____

_____

_____

_____

_____

Open your eyes to all the "hidden treasures" in the natural world. Look at the bark on a tree, the colors on a pigeon's feathers, or the sky's sunny, windy wonders. Or pick up a few fruits and vegetables. Peel an orange. Cut open an apple. Look at the inside of a cabbage leaf or the bottom of a dog's paw. Wonder at the Designer's designs. _____

_____

_____

_____

Do "unpicked raspberries" and "discarded pumpkins" in your life cause you regret? If so, what and why?

_____

_____

_____

Lord, as I Open . . .

MY SENSORS TO THE WONDER OF THIS WORLD—ITS
SIGHTS AND TEXTURES AND CREATURES—REMIND
ME OF YOUR GREATNESS, ABOVE AND BEYOND
ANYTHING I SEE IN YOUR CREATION. THROUGH
JESUS I COME, AMEN.

EACH SUNDOWN IS A BRILLIANT
REFLECTION OF GOD'S PERFECT
ORDER AND TIMING—A WINK
FROM THE FATHER.

"[Jesus,] stay with us, for it is nearly
evening; the day is almost over."
So he went in to stay with them.

LUKE 24:29

CHAPTER 22

OPEN TO THE
BLESSINGS OF SUNSET

Reflection
WAYNE WATSON

I'm partial to sundowns. Watching the sun go down from my backyard is one of my favorite things in all the world. Sundown is a built-in, daily signal from God, reminding us of simple, spiritual truths. It reminds me of three spiritual truths in particular—the need for *reflection*, the need for *rest*, and the promise of the Lord's *return*.

When the sun goes down in the evening and the heat of the day begins to subside, my mind naturally turns toward spiritual matters in a moment of reflection. We all spend too little time reflecting, too little time alone. Solitude gives me time to consider my walk with the Lord in particular and my life walk in general. Gratitude overwhelms me when I ponder the goodness of God. Even when problems must be addressed and dealt with—when mistakes must be acknowledged, regretted, confessed, and forgiven—

even then, thankfulness for God's faithfulness and for all His blessings rises to the top.

Sundown is a good time to call it quits too—a reminder to *rest*. I continue to be amazed at the energy and work ethic of my wife, Lynn. For all our years together, she's been a wife, a homemaker, and a mom. Her job is never done. Still, I try to encourage her to say, at some point in the day, "That's it. I've done enough for today." Back before electricity or other types of artificial light, people had to quit working at sundown—they had no choice; they couldn't see! Perhaps sundown is God's suggestion that we lay down our work and rest for a while. Just a thought.

Sundown also signals something else to me. It reminds me that God is faithful to His promises and that He will return someday to take me home. Growing up, I often heard that Jesus was coming soon, and—I've got to be brutally honest here—that revelation scared me half to death! Beyond being frightened, I was just plain *not excited* about it. I was just beginning to learn about life, and frankly, there were some things I was really looking forward to. I specifically remember praying, and I'm not joking here, "Lord, I know You're coming back soon, but I sure do hope You'll hold off until I get my driver's license!" After the driver's-license stage, I prayed, "Lord, it's me again . . . I know you're coming soon, but I sure would like to get married and have a family before the world comes to an end." Life and years continue to present options, and some of them look pretty good, don't they? But I have to say that as the years go by, life's goodies have become less and less attractive. Earth is not our home. For the Christian man, woman, or child, there will always be an unfulfilled longing for the uninterrupted, eternal presence of the Lord.

With each sundown I remember that God has blessed me with one more day, and I pray that He will give me the capacity and the good sense to live each day in a way that will bring a smile to His face, to light my world, to love the wife He gave me, and to never stop looking for His return. Each sundown is a brilliant reflection of God's perfect order and timing—a wink from the Father saying, "I've not forgotten you . . . peace be with you."

When the sun goes down in your backyard tonight, do a little *reflecting*, allow yourself to *rest*, and turn your eyes toward the heavens as you wait for His *return*.

YOUR FRESH TAKE

Reflect. Rest. Return. Add to this list other words that you connect to sunsets. Turn your additional words into spiritual truths that are meaningful to you.

_____

_____

_____

_____

Every day's sundown provides an opportunity to ponder the faithfulness of God—more faithful than the sun itself. With every sundown this week, pause to reflect and proclaim one way God has proven faithful that day. _____

_____

_____

_____

_____

What emotions accompany your contemplation of Christ's return? If emotions are negative, why? Write or say a short prayer that lays your emotions out before the Lord and ends with the words of Revelation 22:20: "Even so, come, Lord Jesus" (KJV). _____

_____

_____

_____

_____

Lord, as I Open . . .

MY EYES TO THE BEAUTY—AND FAITHFULNESS OF THE DAILY SETTING OF THE SUN, TURN MY THOUGHTS TO YOUR ROLE IN MY LIFE AND WORLD. AS I REFLECT AND THEN REST THROUGH THE NIGHT, REMIND ME TO EAGERLY AWAIT YOUR RETURN. THROUGH YOUR BLESSED SON, AMEN.

THERE IS AN UNCALCULATING,
UNAFFECTED, UNBOUND
EXCITEMENT IN US WHEN
THE SPIRIT IS GIVEN COMPLETE
FREEDOM TO EXPRESS HIMSELF
THROUGH US.

Do not put out the Spirit's fire.

1 THESSALONIANS 5:19

CHAPTER 23

OPEN TO SPONTANEITY

Reflection
LLOYD J. OGILVIE

Recently at a meeting on the Holy Spirit, I asked each of the participants to select a word which would articulate the quality of life he or she wanted to live. Throughout the remainder of the meeting we were to refer to each other by the dynamic description we had selected. I was not surprised that most people chose a word which was quite opposite their natural personalities. We claimed the promise that the Holy Spirit would enable us to be the persons we were meant to be. What do you suppose I chose for myself?

When I became a Christian, a profound personality transformation began. My experience of the Holy Spirit, the indwelling Christ, has continued to liberate me to be a free person—free to love myself and others unconditionally. Daily I must surrender my tendency to caution, reserve, and defensiveness. The Lord's gift to me is to help me be able to give myself away. To fall in love with people and involve myself with spendthrift abandon in their needs. I long to be a completely open, ready-for-anything kind of person. I don't want to resist life in any way. If there has been any progress toward this goal, it is because of the moment-by-moment renewal of the Lord's Spirit in me.

Therefore, the name I have selected for myself is the focus of the kind of person the Spirit has envisioned in my imagination. Spontaneous Lloyd!

I am convinced that an authentic sign that we have become the residence of the Holy Spirit is that we are spontaneous. My working definition of spontaneity is openness, freedom, expectancy, willingness to be surprised, and affirmation of the many-splendored thing we call life. The basic meaning of the word means "that which is done freely, arising from inherent qualities." Its root is from "out of free will." True spontaneity is the result of surrendering our wills to the indwelling Spirit so that the inherent qualities by which we respond to life are His. There is an uncalculating, unaffected, unbound excitement in us when the Spirit is given complete freedom to express Himself through us. . . .

God has so much more to reveal to us each day. So often we miss the beauty around us and the serendipities offered us because of our fearful effort to defend, protect, and preserve ourselves. As a man said, "I have spent all of my life saving myself for something—I don't know what—and have missed the wonderful delight of living while I'm alive." I have determined to do just the opposite. What about you? . . .

Spontaneity is the result of the fire of the Holy Spirit in us. The first step to spontaneous living is to feed that fire with complete trust. "Don't quench the fire!" Paul tells us. The implication of the Greek is "Don't develop a habit of quenching the Spirit." The word *quench*, when used of fire, means to extinguish, to smother, or stifle. Paul does not mean that we can diminish the Spirit of God, but we can extinguish the fire He builds in our hearts or in others. The only way fire can be extinguished is by something outside itself. The apostle is concerned about anything which hinders the free flow of the Spirit in us or in the Christian fellowship.

When the fires of the Holy Spirit are fueled by our willingness, there is an uncontainable enthusiasm for the gospel, our new life in Christ, people, and the wonder of life. Enthusiasm is the key to great living.

Authentic enthusiasm is a gift. It is not the result of human effort. Many of us have tried on our own strength to become enthusiastic people, only to find that we run out of steam. . . .

What then is the secret of a consistent flow of enthusiasm? The fire of the Holy Spirit! Genuine enthusiasm has its unquestionable origin in the indwelling blaze of the Spirit's living in us. Samuel Chadwick, British preacher (1860–1932), said, "Men ablaze are invincible." And I would add . . . spontaneous.

Your Fresh Take

Select a word that describes the "quality of life" you want to live. In what way would this quality round out your personality or compensate for some of your natural flaws? _____

_____

_____

Consider the following comments by Lloyd Ogilvie: "Authentic enthusiasm is a gift"; "When the fires of the Holy Spirit are fueled by our willingness, there is an uncontainable enthusiasm for the gospel, our new life in Christ, people, and the wonder of life." Have you ever tried to generate enthusiasm yourself? How does trying to do it on your own compare to times when enthusiasm has welled up from inside you? Are you willing to receive the gift of enthusiasm? If not, what holds you back? _____

_____

_____

_____

In what habitual ways do you "quench the Spirit"? What does "Do not put out the Spirit's fire" mean for you in personal and specific terms? _____

_____

_____

_____

Lord, as I Open . . .

A WINDOW OF MY HEART TO YOU, GRACE ME WITH
THE GIFT OF ENTHUSIASM. HELP ME BREAK MY OLD
SPIRIT-QUENCHING PATTERNS AND DELIGHT IN A
CHILDLIKE, SPONTANEOUS LOVE FOR LIFE AND FOR
YOU. THROUGH JESUS I PRAY, AMEN.

PART 4

WINDOWS OF GRACE

GOD'S GRACE IS INDEED
MEANT TO BE A
TRANSFORMING GRACE.

As God's chosen people, holy and dearly loved,
clothe yourselves with compassion,
kindness, humility, gentleness and patience.
Bear with each other and forgive whatever
grievances you may have against one another.

COLOSSIANS 3:12–13

CHAPTER 24

OPEN TO
GODLY GRACE

Reflection
JERRY BRIDGES

One day, driving back to the office from an appointment, I was grappling with some difficult circumstances in my life and feeling a bit sorry for myself. But as I drove, I tried to focus my mind on some portions of Scripture and reflect on them rather than on my problems. As I did this, I thought of Colossians 3:12–14. . . .

I had memorized this passage years ago and had reviewed it and reflected on it many times, but that day I saw the passage in a new way. Always before, when reflecting on the passage, my mind had gone directly to the character traits we are to put on: compassion, kindness, humility, gentleness, patience, forbearance, and love. I had never paid attention to the apostle Paul's introductory phrase: "Therefore, as God's chosen people, holy and dearly loved." To me Paul was saying nothing more than, "Since you are

Christians, act like Christians." I saw his emphasis to be solely on Christian duty, the traits of Christ's character I should seek after.

But that day the Holy Spirit caused my mind to focus on the two words "dearly loved." It was as if He said to me, "Jerry, you are feeling sorry for yourself; but the truth is, you are dearly loved by God." Dearly loved by God. What an incredible thought! But it is true, and that afternoon the Holy Spirit drove home to my heart the wonderful truth with such force that my self-pity was completely dispelled. I continued on to our office rejoicing in the fact that, despite my difficult circumstances, I was dearly loved by God.

Of course, the main thrust of Paul's teaching in this passage is that we are to clothe ourselves with Christlike virtues, what I call "garments of grace." But he grounds his exhortation on the grace of God—on the fact that we are chosen by Him, holy in His sight, and dearly loved by Him. It is difficult, perhaps impossible, for us to show compassion or patience to someone else if we are not sure God is patient with us—or, worse, if we don't sense the need for God to be patient with us. So these garments of gracious Christian character can only be put on by those who are consciously experiencing God's grace in their own lives.

Having experienced God's grace, we are then called on to extend that grace to others. The evidence of whether we are living by His grace is to be found in the way we treat other people. If we see ourselves as sinners and totally unworthy in ourselves of God's compassion, patience, and forgiveness, then we will want to be gracious to others.

God's grace is indeed meant to be a transforming grace. As Paul said in Titus 2:11–12, "For the grace of God that brings salvation has appeared to all men. It teaches us to say 'No' to ungodliness and worldly passions, and to live self-controlled, upright and godly lives in this present age." The grace of God brings salvation, not only from the guilt and condemnation of sin, but also from the reign of sin in our lives. It teaches us to say "No" to ungodly character traits, but also to say "Yes" to godly character traits. God's grace teaches us to clothe ourselves with "garments of grace."

YOUR FRESH TAKE

Choose one "garment of grace" listed in Colossians 3:12–14 that is most often missing from your "wardrobe." How does the reminder that you are "dearly loved" influence your ability to "put on" this particular garment?_____

_____

_____

_____

_____

In what area of life do you often slip into a self-pity mode? How does the reminder that you are "dearly loved" influence this frame of mind? _____

_____

_____

_____

_____

What *has* grace transformed in your life? What transformation do you hope grace will continue to affect?

_____

_____

_____

_____

Lord, as I Open . . .

MYSELF TO THE TRANSFORMING POWER OF YOUR
AMAZING LOVE, I MAKE A COMMITMENT TO DRESS
MYSELF WITH THE WARDROBE OF GRACE. DRESSED
IN THAT FINERY, HELP ME TO BE GRACIOUS TO
OTHERS, SHOWING THEM THAT THEY ARE LOVED.
IN CHRIST'S NAME, AMEN.

THEY CHOSE "GLAD" OVER "SAD,"
AND THEY AND THOSE
AROUND THEM WERE THE
RICHER AS A RESULT.

Whatsoever things are lovely, whatsoever things are of good report; if there be any virtue, and if there be any praise, think on these things.

PHILIPPIANS 4:8 KJV

CHAPTER 25

OPEN TO THE
GOOD AND GLAD

Reflection
MARILYN MEBERG

I've always had a particular affinity for the message of that verse because of the way it became part of my childhood experience. My father pastored small rural churches in the state of Washington, and it was his custom to visit his church members' homes at least once every two weeks. Generally, these people lived on farms scattered around the little town of Amboy. To call on just two families often took an entire afternoon.

I loved going on these pastoral calls with my dad. I liked spending time with my father, and I enjoyed riding around in the old Model T Ford, which, much to my mother's chagrin, he had painted purple and yellow. This old eyesore coughed, hissed, and belched with such noisy enthusiasm it made me giggle. (Dad told me he felt the car's basic usefulness was that its sounds warned his parishioners several miles in advance that "the preacher was coming." They had plenty of time to hide whatever needed to be hidden and pull out whatever needed to be seen.)

One of my favorite pastoral calls was to Mr. and Mrs. Wheeler's farm. Mrs. Wheeler was the most pleasant, jolly, and "laughy" lady I've ever known. She was exceedingly heavy and, not surprisingly, a fabulous cook. Her husband, who was not as tall as she and weighed at least one hundred pounds less, called her his "Baby Dumpling." She called him "Mr. Wheeler." They had been married for more than fifty years but spoke to each other with the tenderness of newlyweds. I loved being around them.

Mrs. Wheeler (I wouldn't dare call her Baby Dumpling, even behind her back) habitually interspersed her conversation with the phrase, "I was just thinking whatsoever lovely . . ." For example, she would respond to our noisy entrance onto their property with, "Well, Pastor, I was just thinking whatsoever lovely, and here you are!" or "I was just thinking whatsoever lovely when I decided to make a peach cobbler," or "I was just thinking whatsoever lovely when Mr. Wheeler surprised me with a kiss on the back of my neck."

These statements always seemed to inspire wonderfully contagious moments of laughter from Mrs. Wheeler. It was impossible not to join in, even when nothing about her comments seemed especially funny to me.

Lurching home from the Wheelers' one afternoon, I asked Dad why Mrs. Wheeler said "whatsoever lovely" about so many things. Dad was thoughtful for a minute and then replied, "Well, Marilyn, Mrs. Wheeler has a habit. She told me one time she could either think sad thoughts or glad thoughts, and she would rather think glad ones, or as Scripture says, 'lovely' ones."

It wasn't that Mrs. Wheeler couldn't think of any sad thoughts to consider. I learned some years later that the Wheelers' only child had died of rheumatic fever at the age of six. Apparently, they had made a conscious choice about how they would cope with their loss. They chose "glad" over "sad," and they and those around them were the richer as a result of that choice.

We are all capable of increasing our state of cheerfulness. Being of good cheer is an attitude of the mind made possible by God's enabling power within us. As we remember that Christ, our firm foundation, never moves or wavers, we can, then, in partnership with Him, make choices about our habits of mind that produce attitudes of cheer.

YOUR FRESH TAKE

Read all six "whatsoever" phrases listed in Philippians 4:8. (If possible, read them in several Bible versions.) Which "whatsoever" is hardest for you to "think on"? Why? _____

_____

_____

_____

Has your positive thought life ever directly influenced your attitude and actions toward others? (Think in terms of Colossians 3:12–13, discussed in the previous chapter—your ability or desire to "clothe" yourself "with compassion, kindness, humility, gentleness and patience.") What were the results of your choice to be glad? _____

_____

_____

_____

Discuss one area of your life where you traditionally choose "sad" over "glad" thoughts. To get from sad to glad, what changes in habits or in prayer do you need to make? _____

_____

_____

_____

Lord, I Open . . .

MY THOUGHT LIFE TO THE GOOD AND GLAD. SHOW
ME CLEARLY HOW THIS CHANGE IN ATTITUDE CAN
INFLUENCE MY CONVERSATION AND OPEN CHANNELS
OF GRACE IN MY OWN LIFE AND THE LIVES OF THOSE
AROUND ME. THROUGH JESUS, AMEN.

OUR FAMILY HAS REPEATEDLY
EXPERIENCED RETURNS IN
EXCESS FOR ANY SACRIFICE
OF TIME, ENERGY, MONEY,
OR WEAR AND TEAR
INVOLVED IN HOSPITALITY.

*Offer hospitality to one another without
grumbling. Each one should use whatever
gift he has received to serve others.*

1 PETER 4:9–10

CHAPTER 26

OPEN TO HOSPITALITY

Reflection
MIRIAM HUFFMAN ROCKNESS

Kimberly, you're going to have to move your things out of your room right now. Our company will be here in less than an hour!"

Shifting into high gear, I enter the last stretch of my preparations for overnight guests. I can feel the tension build as I attend to the final details: place clean towels in the bathroom; add fresh bars of soap; put a rocking chair into our makeshift "guest room"; plump the pillows in the living room. . . .

Amidst my inevitable rushed and hectic last-minute preparations, I have no reservations. I'm committed. Underlying the work, stress, and momentary inconvenience of hosting is the privilege of having company. At the start, the very act of opening the door of hospitality presupposes bounty. A roof to shelter, food to share, fellowship to offer are but tangible evidences of one's being blessed.

I first learned this truth on a choir trip when I was in high school. Carefully instructed by our leaders that "service" did not end with the concert but extended into the homes that hosted us, my roommate and I were nonetheless taken aback by the shabby and crowded dwelling to which we were assigned one night. Even the warmth of the hot chocolate served by our elderly hostess could not remove the chill of the Canadian evening from this unheated apartment. Weary from days of travel and evenings of singing, we had to stifle yawns as our hostess produced pictures and tales of her geographically scattered family.

With relief we sank at last into the double bed that filled the tiny room separated from the kitchen by only a curtain. I lay in bed listening to our hostess wash the cups and saucers, straighten the chairs around the table. Finally, the lights were switched off. The only sound was the ticking of a clock. Slipping out of bed to visit the bathroom, I groped my way into the kitchen and stumbled into a large object. I adjusted my focus to the moonlit room. Sound asleep in a straight chair was our hostess, a blanket wrapped around her street clothes! Totally absorbed in the discomfort of our "unlucky draw," it hadn't occurred to me to wonder where *she* was sleeping. "Jean," I whispered, returning to our room, "we have *her* room. She's sitting up all night!"

Early the next morning we woke to the wonderful

aromas of sizzling bacon and English muffins toasting on an oven rack. Two humbled girls sat at the kitchen table trying now to give of ourselves in some small way to one who had given us her rare gift—all that she had. . . .

Blessings received in exchange for hospitality underscore the fundamental biblical principle stressed in the Prayer of Saint Francis: "It is in giving that we receive." Our family has repeatedly experienced returns in excess for any sacrifice of time, energy, money, or wear and tear involved in hospitality. . . .

Potentially, hospitality brings benefits to all involved. In his book *Reaching Out*, Henri Nouwen claimed, "Guest and host alike can reveal their most precious gifts and bring new life to each other." Surely our children's horizons have been stretched beyond the limits of our social, cultural, and racial backgrounds through guests in our home. They have lingered at the table to hear elderly friends recall tales of "when I was young." They have been entertained by anecdotes and skits of visiting speakers unwinding from public ministry. They have been inspired by impromptu performances of guest recitalists. They have been challenged to respond to the needs of hurting and needy people. In short, through hospitality our children—and we parents—have benefited from experiences broader than what one family can provide.

YOUR FRESH TAKE

What keeps you—or others—from practicing hospitality?_____
_____
_____
_____
_____

What past experiences have shown you that "it is in giving that we receive"? _____
_____
_____
_____
_____

Brainstorm ways you could facilitate meeting and conversing with others. List ways you could be hospitable even if you had no extra food budget or could not invite people into your home. _____
_____
_____
_____
_____

Lord, as I Open . . .

MY HOME AND MY LIFE TO OTHERS, HELP ME TO SEE
THAT I AM OPENING MYSELF TO YOU. I ADMIT THAT
SOMETIMES ENTERTAINING SEEMS TO TAKE SO MUCH
EFFORT. I WONDER IF IT'S WORTH THE BOTHER.
SHOW ME THE REWARDS OF OPENING THE DOOR
AND WELCOMING FRIENDS, ACQUAINTANCES, AND
EVEN STRANGERS INTO MY WORLD. AMEN.

THE CHRISTIAN GIVES ALL SHE
KNOWS OF HERSELF TO ALL
SHE KNOWS OF GOD AND
CONTINUES TO GROW IN
THE KNOWLEDGE OF BOTH.

*Grow in the grace and knowledge of
our Lord and Savior Jesus Christ.*

2 PETER 3:18

CHAPTER 27

OPEN TO
FAITH AND FREEDOM

Reflection
GLADYS HUNT

Let me suggest two poor attitudes that cause spiritual paralysis and keep us from moving on with God.

(1) We may have unrealistic expectations that defeat us before we even begin. Being human gives us an in-built tendency to blame others for their imperfections and the distress this causes us. We keep waiting for things to change so we can begin to grow spiritually. Sometimes we try a self-improvement course because we blame ourselves for everything that has gone wrong, and we want to get ourselves in shape to begin to trust God.

The world isn't perfect; our family isn't perfect; our friends aren't perfect; we aren't perfect. None of this takes God by surprise. Why it should surprise sinners that we are imperfect is a mystery. But some Christians can't believe that God has done much until the situation becomes absolute perfection—which it hardly ever does on earth. For instance, a mother can keep peace from flowing through her home while she waits for everyone to shape up. I know of a woman who fussed because her husband stopped at the tavern every night on his way home from work. When he stopped doing that, she fussed because he didn't come to the table at her first call for supper. She forgot all about thanking God that the tavern was no longer an issue.

Another woman I know prayed that God would help her daughter become a better student at school. When the daughter's attitude changed and she moved up to a C average, the mother kept pushing and praying that she would become an A student. Kathleen was not made to be an A student; she was a loving, kind C student. Her mother had unrealistic goals based on her view of how things ought to be rather than on how they actually were. No love, joy, or peace came through from this mother to the family because the fruit of the Spirit wasn't realized in her own life. She didn't recognize God's help when she saw it.

Christians need to learn to live in a real world with real problems, with a real God who is capable of meeting our human needs for time and eternity. And we need to set time against eternity to keep our values straight. In light of eternity much of what we count of supreme worth will be seen as trivia.

The Christian gives all she knows of herself to all she knows of God and continues to grow in the knowledge of both. She becomes a channel for the outflow of His character as she takes on "the shape of Christ." She cannot wait for life to change, but says "The life I now live, I live by faith."

(2) We may have an inadequate concept of freedom, which makes us afraid to give ourselves completely to anyone, least of all to God. The key to giving ourselves to others is our personal abandonment to God. But we are afraid. And so we hold on tightly to ourselves, afraid to lose our life because we are bent on saving it.

Freedom involves living the way we were intended to live, according to our nature. For instance, a train is constructed to run on rails. It experiences freedom only when it accepts the limitations that its nature imposes on it. A train going along the track at full speed is a wonderful sight, but a train attempting to cross a plowed field is a disaster.

Just so with a pianist who accepts the discipline of the keyboard. Her greatest flights of freedom and self-expression are not in defiance of this discipline, but in submission to it.

Who best knows the nature of our freedom? I would sooner give God that wisdom than claim it for myself.

YOUR FRESH TAKE

Consider Gladys Hunt's first cause of spiritual paralysis: unrealistic expectations of others and ourselves. Think of a situation in your past or present life in which expecting perfection has kept you from rejoicing in small victories._____

_____

_____

_____

_____

"We hold on tightly to ourselves, afraid to lose our life because we are bent on saving it." Reflect on this line in terms of this book's theme of "opening." If "opening" yourself to God feels frightening, what are you afraid of losing? _____

_____

_____

_____

_____

Has it been your experience that accepting limitations paradoxically opens a window to freedom? If so, how and why? _____

_____

_____

_____

_____

Lord, as I Open . . .

MYSELF TO LEARNING MORE ABOUT MYSELF, ABOUT
YOU, AND ABOUT THIS WALK OF FAITH, I ASK YOU,
BY YOUR WISDOM AND GRACE, TO LEAD ME INTO
YOUR TRUTH AND THE FREEDOM IT GIVES. IN
JESUS'S NAME, AMEN.

THIS LIFE OF FAITH . . . CONSISTS
IN JUST THIS—BEING A CHILD
IN THE FATHER'S HOUSE.

*For you did not receive a spirit that makes you
a slave again to fear, but you received
the Spirit of sonship. And by him we cry,
"Abba, Father." The Spirit himself testifies with
our spirit that we are God's children.*

ROMANS 8:15–16

CHAPTER 28

OPEN TO
CHILDLIKE REST

Reflection
HANNAH WHITALL SMITH

Do you recollect the delicious sense of rest with which you have sometimes gone to bed at night after a day of great exertion and weariness? How delightful was the sensation of relaxing every muscle and letting your body go in a perfect abandonment of ease and comfort. . . . You trusted yourself to the bed in an absolute confidence, and it held you up, without effort, or strain, or even thought on your part. You rested!

But suppose you had doubted the strength or the stability of your bed, and had dreaded each moment to find it giving way beneath you and landing you on the floor; could you have rested then? Would not every muscle have been strained in a fruitless effort to hold yourself up, and would not the weariness have been greater than not to have gone to bed at all? Let this analogy teach you what it means to rest in the

Lord. Let your souls lie down upon His sweet will, as your bodies lie down in their beds at night. . . .

Take another analogy, which our Lord has abundantly sanctioned—that of the child-life. For Jesus "called a little child and had him stand among them. And he said, 'I tell you the truth, unless you change and become like little children, you will never enter the kingdom of heaven'" (Matthew 18:2–3).

Now what are the characteristics of a little child, and how does he live? He lives by faith, and his chief characteristic is thoughtlessness. His life is one long trust from year's end to year's end. He trusts his parents, he trusts his caretakers, he trusts his teachers, he even trusts people sometimes who are utterly unworthy of trust, because of the confidence in his nature. And his trust is abundantly answered. He provides nothing for himself, and yet everything is provided. He takes no thought for the morrow. . . . He goes in and out of his father's house with an unspeakable ease and abandonment, enjoying all the good things it contains, without having spent a penny in procuring them. . . . He lives in the present moment, and receives his life unquestioningly as it comes to him day by day from his father's hands.

I was visiting once in a wealthy house, where there was one adopted child, upon whom was lavished all the love and tenderness and care that human hearts could bestow, or human means procure. And as I watched that child running in and out day by day, free and lighthearted, with the happy carelessness of childhood, I thought what a picture it was of our wonderful position as children in the house of our Heavenly Father. And I said to myself, *Nothing would so grieve and wound the loving hearts around her, as to see this little child beginning to be worried or anxious about herself in any way—about whether her food and clothes would be provided for her, or how she was to get her education or her future support. How much more must the great, loving heart of our God and Father be grieved and wounded at seeing His children taking so much anxious care and thought*! And I understood why it was that our Lord had said to us so emphatically, "Take no thought for yourselves."

Who is the best cared for in every household? Is it not the little children? And does not the least of all, the helpless baby, receive the largest share? As a late writer has said, the baby "toils not, neither does he spin; and yet he is fed, and clothed, and loved, and rejoiced in," and none so much as he.

This life of faith, then, about which I am writing, consists in just this—being a child in the Father's house. And when this is said, enough is said to transform every weary, burdened life into one of blessedness and rest.

YOUR FRESH TAKE

Summarize what the bed analogy in the reflection says to you. How does this reflect God's grace?

_____

_____

_____

_____

Name qualities of a child who loves a good father enough to relate to him with the innocent intimacy implied in the name Daddy—Abba. Which of these qualities do you exhibit in relationship to your heavenly Father? _____

_____

_____

_____

Of course there is no perfect human father. To "go for" an intimate relationship with the perfect, heavenly Father, what change do you need to be open to?

_____

_____

_____

_____

Lord, as I Open . . .

MY CHILD-HEART TO YOUR FATHER-HEART, SHOW ME
WHAT FAITH INVOLVES, SO I MIGHT LEARN TO REST
IN THE GRACE OF YOUR PERFECT FATHER-LOVE. IN
JESUS'S NAME, AMEN.

PART 5

WINDOWS OF
PURPOSE

You can change your spiritual tires every week, but that won't help unless you submit your life to God on a daily basis.

Submit yourselves, then, to God. Resist the devil, and he will flee from you. Come near to God and he will come near to you. Wash your hands, you sinners, and purify your hearts, you double-minded.

JAMES 4:7–8

CHAPTER 29

OPEN TO
GOD'S ALIGNMENT

Reflection
TONY EVANS

Submission to God requires a new alignment of our lives.

When your tires are out of alignment, you may feel your car pull to one side or the other. At other times you can't detect the problem. But one way you can know your car needs an alignment is when the front tires begin to wear unevenly.

Some Christians look at their lives and see the uneven wear. They may even feel themselves being pulled to one side or the other by the world, the flesh, and the devil. They may be experiencing more defeats than victories. They find themselves unable to cope with the constant battle with sin that Christians must fight every day. They know there's a problem, so they keep changing "tires," hoping to solve it. Let me explain.

Christians who don't feel fully aligned with the Lord may keep changing churches, hoping to find something that can pull them back in proper alignment with God. Or they may go after a certain spiritual experience that promises something new, running from this conference to that seminar in search of help.

But if the front end of your car is out of alignment, changing tires won't fix it because the new tires will simply begin to wear out like the old ones.

The same is true spiritually. You can change your spiritual tires every week, but that won't help unless you submit your life to God on a daily basis. Until you bring your heart into its proper alignment under God's authority, you are still going to be a worn-out believer.

Many of our marriages and personal lives are being worn down by the world, and we think the answer is to change our spiritual tires. We want to change churches, change environments, or even change mates.

If this is your situation, check your alignment. More specifically, if you want to prevent the kinds of problems that come when our lives are not in proper relationship to God, check to see if you are in alignment with the Lord and submitted to His authority.

Submission to God means saying to Him on a day-by-day basis, "Not my will, but Your will be done. I subject my desires to Your desires, my dreams to Your dreams, my purposes and plans to Your purposes and plans." What I am talking about is utterly abandoning yourself to God's control.

Now if you've been lined up with the world, taking your orders from the culture and from your old sinful nature, you'll find it tough to get yourself back in rank under your Commander, Jesus Christ. But this is a necessary first step in experiencing the kind of relationship with God that grows you into maturity and Christlikeness.

Here's another way to look at this issue of submission. You know what it's like to be in bed on a dark, cold winter morning, comfortable in that spot you have warmed up, and hear the alarm go off.

You know what that means. It's time to get up. But that spot in your bed is so warm and comfortable. You're all covered up, and you don't want to be interrupted. You don't want to leave your bed and put your feet on a cold floor.

But you get up anyway. You choose to get out of bed and go to work. Why? Because you know that the rewards of going to work, of earning a living so you can provide the house that holds your warm bed, are greater than the temporary pleasure of a few extra minutes in a warm bed.

Now you may not feel like getting up on that

particular morning. But the price tag for turning over and staying in that warm spot is too high to pay.

Can you see where I'm going? Submitting to God requires the choice (an act of the will) to leave that little warm spot we have developed in the world. I don't know what your "warm spot" is, but most Christians have one.

God is calling us to leave that temporary comfort for the greater reward of getting ourselves in proper rank under Him.

YOUR FRESH TAKE

Read again James 4:7–8: "Submit yourselves, then, to God. Resist the devil, and he will flee from you. Come near to God and he will come near to you. Wash your hands, you sinners, and purify your hearts, you double-minded." How is your double-mindedness most evident to you or to others who know you well?

_____

_____

_____

Have you ever tried to change your circumstances when the real problem was within yourself? If so, what happened? _____

_____

_____

If you were to get a "spiritual alignment," what part of your life would run more smoothly? What changes would be evident?_____

_____

_____

_____

What is God asking you to submit to Him today?

_____

_____

_____

Lord, as I Open . . .

MYSELF TO YOU, I KNOW THIS INVOLVES ALIGNING
MY "VEHICLE" WITH YOUR WILL. I WANT TO STAY
IN BALANCE, UNDER THE SUBMISSION OF YOUR
AUTHORITY. MAKE ME WILLING TO CHANGE.
SHOW ME WHAT YOUR WILL IS DAILY, HOURLY,
TODAY, TOMORROW, NEXT WEEK, NEXT YEAR.
THROUGH CHRIST JESUS I PRAY, AMEN.

THE RICHEST MEANING OF YOUR LIFE
IS CONTAINED IN THE IDEA
THAT CHRIST LOVED YOU ENOUGH
TO GIVE HIS LIFE FOR YOU.

Do not conform any longer to the pattern of this world, but be transformed by the renewing of your mind. Then you will be able to test and approve what God's will is—his good, pleasing and perfect will.

ROMANS 12:2

CHAPTER 30

OPEN TO CLAIMING THE BEST

Reflection
CALVIN MILLER

First of all, and perhaps foundational to [healing of a damaged self], is the necessity of getting the God-view of yourself. Who you are is not determined by how you see yourself. You can speak of the more common things that teach you how God sees you; for instance, you are made in His image and likeness. He also gave you this wonderful world to enjoy. He gave you Holy Scripture to teach you of Himself and guide you through the uncharted seas of your future. All these things are beautiful and true, but there is one more lavish proof that you are special to God. The richest meaning of your life is contained in the idea that Christ loved you enough to give His life for you. . . .

Although you may realize [God's] great love for you from time to time, you still can fall under the burden of stifling low self-esteem. Therefore, you must add to the knowledge that you are special in God's sight, the discipline of retraining your thought habits. Inner self-perceptions are desperately hard to reprogram.

. . . Let me suggest five reinforcing disciplines that can be employed to eliminate negative self-concepts.

1. Prepare spiritually for the day. This can be accomplished by rising early enough to read a devotional passage and to focus on God. Then in the quiet time that follows, review in writing what you believe to be God's overall plan for your life, and particularly for this day. Finally, before you leave the devotional arena, rehearse (commit to memory) such Bible verses as will help you view the positive qualities of God's support of your life. There are many fine scriptures which emphasize our ability to handle life through God's power: Philippians 3:14, 4:13, 4:19, 1:6, are such scriptures.

2. Never leave your dressing mirror until you are satisfied that the best criteria for taste and personal neatness have been achieved. Your clothes and personal grooming will go a long way in determining not only how others see you, but how they relate to you.

3. Force yourself into a positive interchange of some sort with all whom your eyes directly meet. This may be only in the saying of "hello" or "please" and "thank you." It may mean that you need to use some interchange of affirmation or affability as well. But the discipline will need to be thorough if you have established an aloof lifestyle.

4. *Make all of life a game of names.* Use your name first when meeting someone for the first time, as it is the best encourager for people to respond by sharing their own. As much as possible, use the names of others in all exchanges. Names are the truly magic words. Then keep at the front of your mind the notion that people are nameable, knowable, and special. The remembering of names is a discipline that will win you much admiration.

5. *Practice the art of peripheral praying for those you see but do not have the time or opportunity to talk with.* Peripheral praying draws your world near and closes a circle of manageability around your acquaintances. It makes you a participant in the whole world. Merely seeing others makes you see yourself in a contextual way. This keeps you from insulating yourself and feeling like a social misfit.

Notice that points one and five are "en-static"; that is, these are ways we deal inside ourselves to help heal our damaged feelings. Points two through four are "ek-static." They are points that bring us joy merely because we are making an effort to get outside ourselves and relate. There is no magic in these ideas. Joy ever relates from the "ecstasy" of standing outside ourselves. Thus, we escape the littleness of our own world.

YOUR FRESH TAKE

What evidence do you have that God loves you? Consider your daily devotional practice. What changes might make you more aware of God's presence in your life and His purpose for you?_____

_____

_____

_____

_____

How do you respond to someone who remembers your name after an initial introduction? Why do you think remembering names is so important? Consider Isaiah 43:1, 6–7._____

_____

_____

_____

_____

Discuss several other "en-static" and "ek-static" ways to claim God's best for your life. _____

_____

_____

_____

_____

Lord, as I Open . . .

MYSELF TO THE LIGHT OF CHRIST, SHOW ME YOUR
PURPOSE FOR ME. DRAW ME OUT OF THE LITTLE-
NESS OF MYSELF INTO THE JOY OF THE WIDER WORLD
YOU'VE CREATED WITH INFINITE LOVE. THROUGH
CHRIST, AMEN.

THE PICTURE OF THE SOUL
THESE GOALS CAPTURE
IS A SOUL THAT IS INTIMATE
WITH GOD.

*Forgetting what is behind and straining
toward what is ahead, I press on toward
the goal to win the prize for which God
called me heavenward in Christ Jesus.*

PHILIPPIANS 3:13–14

CHAPTER 31

OPEN TO
ADVENTURES WITH GOD

Reflection
VALERIE BELL

I added some soul goals to my dreams. Here they are:

1. *I want to delight God*. Scriptures say that God's eyes scan the earth searching for those whose hearts are right toward Him. I desire to be one of those with whom He can consistently find comfort and pleasure. I want to "make His day" as Noah did. Even in a dark day, God found pleasure in Noah. That is the kind of relationship I want with God. I want Him to find comfort with me and experience delight when He thinks about me. I want to learn to hear God's holy laughter regarding me. I want that delight in life that only an open, intimate relationship with God can give.

2. *I want to "practice heaven" by enjoying God now*. The *Westminster Catechism* declares that the chief end of humankind is to glorify God and enjoy Him forever. I want to experience the pleasure of knowing

God with greater intensity as I age. I want my soul to become skilled and comfortable in the practice of heaven—praising and enjoying God. I'm acclimating my eternal soul, my intrinsic self, to the values of heaven now.

3. *I want to have a part in advancing God's kingdom.* Nothing would please me more than knowing I had seriously thwarted the destructive plans of the Evil One. I want there to be no doubt about which side benefited from my loyalties. Understand, I am not envisioning some kind of Joan of Arc role here. I am not wanting to be grandiose or spiritually ambitious. But I want to be increasingly available and skilled for the part God might want me to play in His holy drama.

4. *I want to remain open to the unexpected, off-the-beaten-path plans of God for my life.* I intend to nurture an adventuresome spirit. Why not be open to things in my sixties that I would not consider at a younger age? Forget the small shockers like spitting and picking flowers from other people's gardens. I want to drape my soul in purple and be open to experiencing mission work in Kenya at sixty or a house filled with children at seventy. I want to develop an eagerness for the unconventional, path-less-traveled life. I am not motivated by the shock appeal, however, but by the awareness that God can use people whose boundaries with Him are unconventional and well off the beaten path.

5. *I want to grow in loving graciousness in my relationships*. I want to mellow toward others as I age. I want to be remembered as a truly loving person, not a tough, old bird! I would like to become more of a safe place for the people in my life. I would like my connections with others to be increasingly marked by compassion and an ability to connect with others soul to soul.

6. *I want to laugh more.* I just like the way a laugh rings in the face of evil. There is a holy craziness to an aging woman who can still laugh. "I have confidence in God!" is what that kind of laughter communicates. I love that!

7. *I want to think less like a victim and more like a survivor.* I have some significant life wounds by this point. Don't we all? But I want to feel that I have done more than suffered with these pains. I want to know that I have turned them into learning experiences, builders of interior character. I want to experience "beauty for ashes" as I review the unfolding of my life. May my life deepen, not wither because of painful life experiences.

8. *I want to reaffirm my desire to excel in prayer!* I want my aging to be impacted by contact and communion with God. May I become more astute at hearing God's voice and seeing things, not just from a human perspective but from God's perspective.

The picture of the soul these goals capture is a soul that is intimate with God.

Your Fresh Take

Review Valerie Bell's eight soul goals. If these were your long-term spiritual goals, prioritize them: one through eight. You might prioritize in two different ways: (1) in the order of what you most value or (2) in order of what you think you most *need* or lack.

_____
_____
_____
_____

Write or discuss one or two spiritual goals of your own—thinking in terms of desiring a "wonder-filled future." (Or reword a few of Valerie Bell's goals so they better suit you.) _____
_____
_____
_____
_____

Choose one soul goal, and make a conscious effort to make it a reality today, then tomorrow and tomorrow.

_____
_____
_____
_____

Lord, as I Open . . .

MY SIGHTS TO THE POSSIBILITIES OF MY SOUL GOALS,
WORK YOUR WONDER IN MY LIFE. AS I AGE, MAY MY
RELATIONSHIP WITH YOU GROW MORE INTIMATE,
MY PURPOSE MORE CLEAR, MY COUNTENANCE
MORE CHRISTLIKE. THROUGH HIM, AMEN.

I CAN'T DO MUCH ABOUT CHANGING THE WORLD, BUT . . . I CAN DO SOMETHING ABOUT BRINGING GOD'S PRESENCE INTO THE WORLD IN WHICH HE HAS PUT ME.

We are God's workmanship, created in Christ Jesus to do good works, which God prepared in advance for us to do.

EPHESIANS 2:10

CHAPTER 32

OPEN TO COMPASSIONATE MINISTRY

Reflection
WARREN WIERSBE

Things change, old problems fade, and new problems take their place, but life goes on; and you and I have but one life to live and a job to do for God before it ends. I can't do much about changing the world, but that doesn't keep me awake at night. Even the people in authority can't do much about changing the world. *But I can do something about bringing God's presence into the world in which He has put me, and that's what ministry is all about. . . .*

Years ago I read a fable about an ant who asked a centipede, "How do you know which leg to move next?" The centipede pondered the question and replied, "I guess I've never thought about it." But the more he thought about the question, the more perplexed he became until finally he was so confused he couldn't walk at all.

We can get so wrapped up in pondering the

perplexities of the future ("Which leg shall I move first?") that we fail to seize the opportunities of the present and do the work that's needed right now. Like the professional student who's dying by degrees, we're always learning how to get ready. Somebody asked the father of such a career student, "What's your son going to be when he graduates from the university?" The father replied, "An old man."

All of God's people are ministers; a few are Ministers with a capital *M*. We are either good ministers or bad ministers; but ministers we are, and as ministers we shall be judged by the Lord on the last day. On that day, it won't matter how much we knew, but what we did with what we knew. *Were we loving channels through whom the divine resources could come? Did we meet the needs of others to the glory of God?*

I'm encouraged about the future because God is in it and Jesus promised that the gates of hell would not prevail against His church. The future is our friend when Jesus is our Lord. He still goes before His sheep and prepares the way. Our job isn't to second-guess Him but to follow Him. He'll take care of the rest: "Known to God from eternity are all His works" (Acts 15:18 NKJV).

. . . It has always taken courage and compassion for God's people to minister in any age. The sovereignty of God and the love of God make an unbeatable combination for any servant of God, against which the devil has no power.

So, start ministering today, and keep ministering as long as you can. There is no discharge in this war. God has been our "dwelling place in all generations" (Psalm 90:1 NKJV), and He isn't about to change and desert us. If Jesus doesn't return in our lifetimes, you and I will pass off the scene and probably be forgotten. No matter. If we've done the will of God, we've helped prepare the way for the next generation, just as others prepared the way for us.

The work goes on.

And John Wesley's dying words were right on target for today's church: "The best of all is, God is with us!"

YOUR FRESH TAKE

In your own words define "what ministry is all about." Give examples of how you've found that ministry requires "courage and compassion." Think of what ministry you sense God is calling you to in the near future. What new courageous steps is God asking you to take?_____

_____

_____

_____

_____

Consider the story of the centipede who became paralyzed when he overanalyzed his life. Is there one area of your life where overanalysis (of the past, present, or future) tends to "shut you in" or "shut you down"? How would your decision to step out in faith change this area of your life? _____

_____

_____

_____

_____

What makes you encouraged about the future?

_____

_____

_____

_____

Lord, as I Open . . .

MYSELF TO COMPASSIONATE MINISTRY IN YOUR NAME, SHOW ME THE WORK YOU WANT ME TO DO HERE AND NOW. I CAN'T CHANGE THE WHOLE WORLD, BUT I DO WANT TO BRING YOUR PRESENCE INTO MY SMALL WORLD. GIVE ME STRENGTH FOR TODAY. GIVE ME HOPE FOR TOMORROW—BECAUSE YOU ARE WITH ME. IN JESUS'S NAME, AMEN.

OUR PRAISE CLUSTERS IN CHURCH
AND IN PERSONAL DEVOTIONS;
IT DOES NOT SPREAD
THROUGHOUT OUR LIVES.

Let them give thanks to the LORD
for his unfailing love
and his wonderful deeds for men.
Let them . . . tell of his works
with songs of joy.

PSALM 107:21–22

CHAPTER 33

OPEN TO
JOYFUL WITNESS

Reflection
TIM STAFFORD

I heard an old man, who seemed to overflow with joy and thanksgiving, say that his life had taken a turn when he committed himself to witness every day. By "witness" he did not mean an evangelistic appeal; he meant praising the Lord, "telling of His excellent greatness." He would not let a day go by without telling *someone*—Christian or non-Christian—of God's goodness. Such daily praise opens up a deeper perception of God, and thus to more praise. For praise leads to praise. It may feel awkward at first, but you get the hang of it.

We learn best, I believe, in the company of others. Many (like me) who find it awkward to praise God publicly, find great freedom in congregational singing. There individual contribution is entirely submerged. We make an effort to blend with other voices and to sing together as a single voice. We want to sing as well as we can, but not to draw attention to ourselves. We want to draw attention—especially our own—to the beauty of the song and thus to its object, our Father. Perhaps this is why biblical worship, from the Psalms clear through Paul's "psalms and hymns and spiritual songs," is very musical. Choral singing is one activity in which many people can overcome their stiffness and lose themselves in praise.

But music is not by any means the only way we learn to praise from a group experience. A church worship service is a planned experiment in group praise, in which individuals learn how to praise by being part of a group which does it naturally and harmoniously. The experiment need not stop when we leave the church. I learned how to praise other people by being part of [my wife] Popie's circle. They infected me with their spontaneous environment of praise. The people of God, wherever I meet them, ought to infect me with that same kind of environment, with praise directed not merely toward each other but toward God.

We often miss this crucial link. As a group we praise in church—at least we sing hymns and recite words meant to express praise. As individuals we praise in private. But in between those two experiences we are often too shy to say anything in praise of God, whether at work, in the hardware store, at the movie, or over dinner. Our praise clusters in church and in personal devotions; it does not spread throughout our lives.

Thus, not surprisingly, our sense of Jesus's presence tends to be restricted to church and devotions, rather than spreading through all of our life.

I am not suggesting that we become people who spout "Praise the Lord" at every opportunity. Such praise may be, like flattery, thoughtless or contrived—not really praise at all, just religious words meant to reassure ourselves. Rather, I wish we could form covenants together, whether as friends or members of churches and Bible studies, to learn to praise God thoughtfully at every opportunity. Such praise would be highly varied, as we are varied people. It need not, I think, be contrived or embarrassing to others. Most importantly, this continuance of praise could help make our lives into one whole piece: instruments of praise saying aloud what is surely the Truth above all truths. Great is the Lord, and greatly to be praised.

YOUR FRESH TAKE

Recall times when someone else's joyful witness has spoken to your heart. _____
_____
_____
_____
_____

From what you have observed of your family, friends, or strangers praising you or others, what have you learned about praising God? In what other ways have you learned to praise God?_____
_____
_____
_____
_____

What "joyful witness" do others see in you or hear from you? If it's hard for you to answer this, how can you open yourself to joyful witness?_____
_____
_____
_____
_____

Lord, I Open . . .

MY SPIRIT AND LIFT MY VOICE TO WITNESS TO YOUR "EXCELLENT GREATNESS." HELP ME SEE WAYS TO DO THIS EVERY DAY—TO TELL SOMEONE OF YOUR GOODNESS. THROUGH CHRIST I PRAY, AMEN.

WHEN WE ARE THAT HOLY
COMMUNITY, WE MAKE AN IMPACT
ON AN UNHOLY WORLD,
NO MATTER HOW DESPERATE THE
CIRCUMSTANCES.

Let your light shine before men, that
they may see your good deeds and
praise your Father in heaven.

MATTHEW 5:16

CHAPTER 34

OPEN TO
HOLY WITNESS

Reflection
CHARLES COLSON

To model the kingdom of God in the world, the church must not only be a repentant community, committed to truth, but also a holy community.

The Judeo-Christian heritage is distinguished from all other religions by its covenant with a personal God who chose to dwell in the midst of His people. "I will dwell among the Israelites and be their God," said the Lord (Exodus 29:45). In Hebrew the word *dwell* meant "to pitch a tent"; God said He would pitch His holy tabernacle in the midst of the tents of the Israelites. In the New Testament we read "the Word became flesh, and dwelt among us" (John 1:14). Here also the word *dwelt* in the Greek is translated "to pitch a tent." The covenant, both old and new, is that the God of Abraham, Isaac, and Jacob, the God who later became flesh in Christ, actually dwells in the presence of His people. And thus it is that the central requirement of our faith is that we be holy, for a holy God lives in our midst.

The apostle Peter echoed this theme when he said: "You are a chosen people, a royal priesthood, a holy nation, a people belonging to God" (1 Peter 2:9).

The church is to be a community reflecting God's passion for righteousness, justice, and mercy. When we are that holy community, we make an impact on an unholy world, no matter how desperate the circumstances.

Thousands of such communities of light exist around the world in accountable fellowships where the gospel is faithfully proclaimed and where members reach out in an effort to bring God's mercy and justice to those around them. But my most vivid impressions of the church shining forth have come from some of the darkest places on earth—from prisons around the world. In some ways these fellowships bear real similarity to the monastic outposts—believers faithfully preserving the gospel as those around them sink into depravity.

One such community of light is in Zambia. There in an old colonial-era stockade emaciated inmates, wearing only loincloths, are crowded into primitive, filthy cells where they have to take turns sleeping, since there is not room for them all to lie on the floor at the same time. At night the prisoners are given a bucket of water, after they drink the water, the same bucket is used to carry off their waste in the morning.

When I visited this prison, I was with Rajan, a Christian brother and former inmate at that prison, now chairman of Prison Fellowship Zambia. He led me to a maximum-security compound within the main block. "Listen," he whispered as we got closer. "They're singing."

Guards unlocked a pair of heavy gates, and we stepped into a dusty courtyard ringed by tiny cells. There to welcome us were sixty or seventy radiantly smiling inmates; they stood at the end of the yard before a whitewashed wall, singing praises to God in beautiful harmony. Behind them on the wall was a huge charcoal drawing of Christ on the cross: Jesus the prisoner who shared their suffering and gave them hope and joy in this awful place, where they had come to Christ. . . .

Several years ago I visited Peru's Lurigancho, the largest prison in the world, arriving just a few days after a riot in which several nuns had been taken hostage by the prisoners; one had been killed. . . .

As I toured the block, I came to other cells of light in that dark place, where the smiles of Christian inmates told the story of their utter transformation. The dramatic contrast of this community of gentle Christians, loving and encouraging one another in this hole of violence and hatred, was unforgettable. It was light shining in the darkness. . . .

In prison the contrast is sharp between dark and light. Choices for Christian inmates are usually clear-cut. Yet most of us in the mainstream of Western culture live in shades of gray. It's comfortable to adopt the surrounding cultural values. Yet stand apart we must.

YOUR FRESH TAKE

How does the holy God influence your own Christian witness? The witness of your Christian community?

Think of one specific circumstance when the holy, Christlike witness of the church made an impact on you or your family or your neighborhood. Thank God for that witness and reflection of who He is.

This week how can you resist the impulse to "hide" your light and instead "open a window shade" and let your light shine before others in your home or community?

Lord, as I Open . . .

MYSELF TO YOUR HOLINESS AND ALLOW MYSELF TO
REFLECT THE LIGHT OF CHRIST, FILL MY BEING WITH
COURAGE AND RENEWED VISION FOR THE WORK
OF YOUR KINGDOM. MAY YOUR WILL BE DONE IN
AND THROUGH ME, JUST AS YOUR WILL IS DONE IN
HEAVEN, AMEN.

TO EVERY CRY FROM YOUR
PASSION-FILLED HEARTS,
GOD REPLIES, "CHRIST."

*We continually remember before our God
and Father your work produced by
faith, your labor prompted by love,
and your endurance inspired by hope
in our Lord Jesus Christ.*

1 THESSALONIANS 1:3

CHAPTER 35

OPEN TO
GODLY PASSION

Reflection
LARRY CRABB JR.

To believe Christ (faith), to serve Christ (love), and to wait for Christ (hope): that is what it means to find God.

But to the degree that you haven't found Him, your passions are out of control. Trust is out. You want to explain and control; therefore, you reduce mystery to manageable categories and attempt to run your own life without depending on Christ.

You like to be right. You call it earnestly contending for the faith, and you persuade yourself that you are God's ally in defending truth. But your angry spirit of smugness and condescension gives you away. Compassion and humility yield to arrogance.

You long to *heal*, to relieve pain. But when that becomes a higher priority than worship, you create a god who suits your humane purpose, and you devote your life to helping people feel better about themselves. You end up using a false god rather than worshiping the true One.

You long to *connect* with the supernatural. You embrace mystery, fall prostrate before God in humility, and yield yourself to no higher purpose than experiencing Him. But your focus is on experience. You demand it. So you come up with methods to get it. Eventually, you become more caught up with your theology of finding God and the evidence that you have done so than with God Himself.

To every cry from your passion-filled hearts, God replies, "Christ."

Let your *passion to explain* become a *passion to know Christ* and all that He reveals through the book that God wrote about Him. Think hard, explore, take risks in your ideas, talk to people about their lives, but never leave the chair by the fire for very long. Let your work of faith be always to believe He is good.

Let your *passion to be right* become a *passion to honor Christ* in all that you do. Study hard, dialogue, debate, but always do it in a way that helps others to see how kind and good God really is. Let warm conviction replace cold dogmatism. Let your labor of love be to reflect God's character always.

Let your *passion to heal* become a *passion to give hope*. The wounds won't all go away now. No method or group or counselor can completely heal them. But you can continue on, doing the work of faith and carrying out the labor of love, even though you are still wounded. A better city awaits you. With the patience of hope, serve faithfully now because you know what lies ahead. Don't wait for your wounds to be healed before you serve.

Let your *passion to connect* become a *passion to trust* a sovereign Christ who will do for you exactly what needs to be done. He will reveal the Father in His time and in His way in response to your work of faith, labor of love, and patience of hope.

Most of us are crawling about in a stuffy attic, trying to explain life, demanding to be right, doing our best to relieve pain, and wondering where God is. It is time to find our way back to the living room and into the Father's arms, where we can listen to His Spirit tell the story of Christ.

YOUR FRESH TAKE

With which of the four negative passions (to explain, to be right, to heal, to connect) do you most closely identify? Do you have any insight into why this "passion" is part of your character?_____

_____

_____

_____

_____

Consider the positive passion that corresponds to your reflection in the first question. What new attitudes or actions would this passion bring out in you?

_____

_____

_____

_____

What would it mean for you to stop "crawling about in a stuffy attic" and find your way to the Father's arms?

_____

_____

_____

_____

Lord, as I Open . . .

MYSELF TO GODLY PASSIONS, LET MY WORK BE
PRODUCED BY FAITH. LET MY LABOR BE PROMPTED
BY LOVE. LET MY ENDURANCE BE INSPIRED BY HOPE
IN JESUS CHRIST MY LORD. IN JESUS'S NAME, AMEN.

CLOSING PRAYER

MAX LUCADO

DEAR FATHER,

We pray that You have been blessed by these pages of prayer. We pray that You've been honored by our praise. And Father, we don't intend to stop praising with the closing of this book.

Lord, we are looking forward with great anticipation to our reunion with You. We are ready, O Father, for You to come. We invite You to interrupt this moment with the opening of the heavens.

Open the skies and let the glory of Jesus fall down upon this earth. Come again into time; interrupt it with eternity, and let us stand before You.

Father, let us be caught up with those who will worship You forever. And Lord, we submit this request to You because we know that at the right time You will come; we know that at the right time You will call.

Until that day, we pledge, O Father, to stand in

Your presence, to pray and to praise and to worship You, held to You not by our goodness but by Yours. Empowered by Your Spirit, covered in the goodness of Your Son, adopted by the Father, held close in You.

And Father, may we have the privilege of opening windows everywhere we go. Let Your light pour in, Father, and may Your name be praised.

In Jesus we pray, amen.

CONTRIBUTORS

VALERIE BELL is a conference speaker and the author of *Getting Out of Your Kids' Faces and into Their Hearts* and *She Can Laugh at the Days to Come*.

PAUL BRAND, a missionary surgeon known for his brilliant work in hand surgery, pioneered research on leprosy in India. With Philip Yancey he wrote *Fearfully and Wonderfully Made* and *In His Image*.

JERRY BRIDGES has been on the staff of The Navigators Collegiate Ministries since 1955, serving as a vice president for fifteen of those years. Among his books are *Transforming Grace*, *The Pursuit of Holiness*, and *The Practice of Godliness*.

CHARLES W. COLSON, former special counsel to President Nixon, is chairman of Prison Fellowship Ministries and the author of several books including *Born Again*, *Loving God*, and *How Now Shall We Live?*

CONTRIBUTORS

LARRY CRABB is a distinguished professor at Colorado Christian University and the author of several books, including *The Silence of Adam*, *Inside Out*, and *The Safest Place on Earth*.

ELISABETH ELLIOT returned to Ecuador as a missionary to the very tribe that killed her husband Jim. She has authored several books, including *These Strange Ashes* and *God's Guidance*, and she hosts the *Gateway to Joy* radio program.

TONY EVANS, pastor of Oak Cliff Bible Fellowship in Dallas, and president of the Urban Alternative, is the featured speaker on the radio program *Alternative with Dr. Tony Evans*. A popular inspirational speaker and author, his books include *The Perfect Christian* and *Who Is This King of Glory?*

KEN GIRE, a freelance writer, is the author of several books, including *Moments with the Savior*; *Thanks, Dad, for Teaching Me Well*; and *Reflections on the Word*.

JOHN GUEST, an evangelist for more than thirty years, has taught in Russia, Cuba, Romania, Albania, and Israel. He ministers to a group of believers in Sewickley, Pennsylvania. His books include *Finding Deeper Intimacy with God* and *This World Is Not My Home*.

CYNTHIA HEALD is known for her popular Bible studies: *Becoming a Woman of Excellence*, *Becoming a Woman of Freedom, Becoming a Woman of Purpose,* and *Becoming a Woman of Prayer.*

GLADYS HUNT, a lecturer and conference speaker, is the author of several books, including *Honey for a Child's Heart* and *Persuaded Heart.*

BILL HYBELS is pastor of Willow Creek Community Church in South Barrington, Illinois. He is the author of many books, including *Fit to Be Tied, Too Busy Not to Pray, The God You're Looking For,* and *Making Life Work.*

DENNIS JERNIGAN, known for his ability to usher others into the presence of God through his music, leads a ministry centered on the promise that God's mercy is for everyone, regardless of their past. He also wrote *A Mystery of Majesty* and *This Is My Destiny,* devotional books based on his albums of the same titles.

MAX LUCADO serves as minister of the Oak Hills Church in San Antonio, Texas. His many books include *No Wonder They Call Him the Savior, He Still Moves Stones, Cure for the Common Life,* and *God Came Near.*

CATHERINE MARSHALL was the author of inspirational and fictional bestsellers, including *Something More, Adventures in Prayer, Christy,* and *Julie.*

JIM MCGUIGGAN, born in Belfast, Ireland, has studied and taught Bible at the undergraduate and graduate levels. He works with a congregation near Belfast and has written several books, including his trilogy: *The God of the Towel*; *Jesus, Hero of Thy Soul*; and *Where the Spirit of the Lord Is*.

MARILYN MEBERG, a former professor and counselor, is a speaker for Women of Faith conferences. Her books include *I'd Rather Be Laughing* and *Choosing the Amusing*.

CALVIN MILLER, pastor and professor, is the author of several books, including *Hunger for Meaning*, *Disarming the Darkness*, *An Owner's Manual for the Unfinished Soul*, and *The Singer* trilogy.

LLOYD JOHN OGILVIE is the former chaplain of the U.S. Senate and the author of numerous books, including *God's Best Gift for My Life*, *One Quiet Moment*, *Conversation with God*, and *Facing the Future without Fear*.

LEANNE PAYNE founded Pastoral Care Ministries, which promotes the ministry of healing prayer. She earned her master's degrees from Wheaton College and the University of Arkansas and has written several books, including *Restoring the Christian Soul* and *Listening Prayer*.

MIRIAM HUFFMAN ROCKNESS is the author of *Keep These Things—Ponder Them in Your Heart*; *Home—God's Design*; and *A Passion for the Impossible*, a biography of artist and missionary Lilias Trotter.

LUCI SHAW, known for her poetry, is the author of several books, including *God in the Dark*, *Writing the River*, and *Water My Soul*.

GARY SMALLEY, president of Today's Family, is a popular speaker and the author of a number of books, including *Love Is a Decision*, *Making Love Last Forever*, and *Forever Love*.

HANNAH WHITALL SMITH, raised a Quaker, was influential in the nineteenth-century Keswick movement. Her classic, *The Christian's Secret of a Happy Life*, is one of the best-selling Christian books of all time.

TIM STAFFORD serves as a senior writer for *Christianity Today* magazine. He coedited *The Student Bible* with Philip Yancey, and his books include *Knowing the Face of God* and *A Thorn in the Heart*.

CHARLES SWINDOLL is pastor of Stonebriar Community Church. A popular Bible teacher on *Insight for Living*, he is the author of many books, including *Classic Truths for Triumphant Living* and *Dropping Your Guard*.

JONI EARECKSON TADA, founder and president of JAF Ministries—an organization that accelerates Christian outreach in the disability community—is an artist and the best-selling author of many books, including *Joni*, *God's Precious Love*, and *Holiness in Hidden Places*.

CORRIE TEN BOOM was sent to Ravensbruck concentration camp for hiding Jews in her native Holland. After World War II she traveled the world telling her story. Her bestseller, *The Hiding Place*, is also a feature movie.

JEFF WALLING is a sought-after speaker, lecturing to tens of thousands annually at Christian universities, evangelism seminars, and conferences worldwide. He is the author of *Daring to Dance with God* and *Until I Return*.

SHEILA WALSH, recording artist and former cohost of *The 700 Club*, is a featured speaker for Women of Faith conferences. She is the author of several books, including *Gifts for Your Soul*, *Honestly*, and *Bring Back the Joy*.

WAYNE WATSON has had thirty-four top ten singles, twenty-one of them reaching number one. He has been nominated for sixteen Dove awards and three Grammy awards, and he has won four Dove awards. He also authored a devotional book with the same title as his album *The Way Home*.

THELMA WELLS, president of A Woman of God Ministries in Dallas, is a popular Women of Faith conference speaker and the author of several books, including *Bumblebees Fly Anyway*, *Destiny and Deliverance*, and *God Will Make a Way*.

CONTRIBUTORS

WARREN WIERSBE, is a former pastor at Moody Church in Chicago. For ten years he was the general director of the *Back to the Bible* radio ministry. He is a popular speaker and a prolific author, having written over one hundred books. Some of his books include: the "Be" series, *Being a Child of God*, *Pause for Power*, *Prayer 101*, as well as a Bible Exposition Commentary.

PHILIP YANCEY is editor at large for *Christianity Today* and the best-selling author of many books, including *What's So Amazing about Grace? The Jesus I Never Knew*, and *The Bible Jesus Read*.

RAVI ZACHARIAS is president of Ravi Zacharias International Ministries in Norcross, Georgia. His many books include *Can Man Live Without God? Deliver Us from Evil*, and *Cries of the Heart*.

ACKNOWLEDGMENTS

REFLECTIONS LISTED
BY CHAPTER NUMBER

Introduction. Taken from *Opening Windows* (sound recording). Copyright © 1998 by Here to Him Music. Used by permission of Here to Him Music.

1. Taken from *In Search of Wonder* edited by Lynn Anderson. Copyright © 1995 by Howard Books. Used by permission of the publisher.

2. Taken from *A Closer Walk* by Catherine Marshall. Copyright © 1986 by Calen, Inc. Used by permission of Chosen Books, a division of Baker Books.

3. Taken from *A Mystery of Majesty* by Dennis Jernigan. Copyright © 1997 by Dennis Jernigan. Used by permission of Howard Books.

4. Taken from *Daring to Dance with God* by Jeff Walling. Copyright © 1996 by Jeff Walling. Used by permission of Howard Books.

5. Taken from *Gifts for Your Soul* by Sheila

Walsh. Copyright © 1997 by Sheila Walsh. Used by permission of Zondervan.

6. Taken from *Cries of the Heart* by Ravi Zacharias. Copyright © 1998 by Ravi Zacharias. W Publishing Group, Nashville, Tennessee. All rights reserved. Used by permission of the publisher.

7. Taken from *Heaven, Your Real Home* by Joni Eareckson Tada. Copyright © 1995 by Joni Eareckson Tada. Used by permission of Zondervan.

8. Taken from *God Will Make a Way* by Thelma Wells. Copyright © 1998 by Thelma Wells. Used by permission of Thomas Nelson Publishers.

9. Taken from *Don't Wrestle, Just Nestle* by Corrie ten Boom. Copyright © 1978 by Corrie ten Boom. Used by permission of Fleming H. Revell, a division of Baker Books.

10. Taken from *I Was Just Wondering* by Philip Yancey. Copyright © 1989, 1998 by Wm. B. Eerdmans Publishing Co. Used by permission of the publisher.

11. Taken from *Only a Prayer Away* by John Guest. Copyright © 1985 by John Guest. Published by Servant Publications. Used by permission of the author.

12. Taken from *Growing Strong in the Seasons of Life* by Charles Swindoll. Copyright © 1983 by Charles R. Swindoll, Inc. Used by permission of Zondervan.

13. Taken from *Listening Prayer* by Leanne

Payne. Copyright © 1994 by Leanne Payne. Used by permission of Baker Books.

14. Taken from *A Woman's Journey to the Heart of God* by Cynthia Heald. Copyright © 1997 by Cynthia Heald. Used by permission of Thomas Nelson Publishers.

15. Taken from *Too Busy Not to Pray* by Bill Hybels. Copyright © 1998 by Bill Hybels. Used with permission from InterVarsity Press, P.O. Box 1400, Downers Grove, IL 60515.

16. Taken from *Joy That Lasts* by Gary Smalley with Al Janssen. Copyright © 1986 by Gary T. Smalley. Used by permission of Zondervan.

17. Taken from *Jesus, Hero of Thy Soul* by Jim McGuiggan. Copyright © 1998 by Jim McGuiggan. Used permission of Howard Books.

18. Taken from *Keep a Quiet Heart*, © 1995 by Elisabeth Elliot. Published by Servant Publications, Box 8617, Ann Arbor, Michigan, 48107. Used by permission of the publisher.

19. This material is taken from *God's Forever Feast*, by Paul Brand © 1998. Used by permission of Discovery House Publishers, Box 3566, Grand Rapids, Michigan 49501. All rights reserved.

20. Taken from *Windows of the Soul* by Ken Gire. Copyright © 1996 by Ken Gire Jr. Used by permission of Zondervan.

21. Taken from *Water My Soul* by Luci Shaw.

Copyright © 1998 by Luci Shaw. Used by permission of Zondervan Books.

22. Taken from *The Way Home* by Wayne Watson. Copyright © 1998 by Wayne Watson. Used by permission of Howard Books.

23. Taken from *Life As It Was Meant to Be* by Lloyd J. Ogilvie. Copyright © 1980 by Regal Books. Used by permission of the author.

24. Reprinted from *Transforming Grace*. Copyright © 1991 by Jerry Bridges. Used by permission of NavPress, Colorado Springs, CO. All rights reserved. For copies call (800) 366-7788.

25. Taken from *I'd Rather Be Laughing* by Marilyn Meberg. Copyright © 1998 by Marilyn Meberg. W Publishing Group, Nashville, Tennessee. All rights reserved. Used by permission of the publisher.

26. Taken from *Home: God's Design by Miriam Huffman Rockness*. Copyright © 1990 by Miriam Huffman Rockness. Published by Zondervan. Used by permission of the author.

27. Taken from *A Persuaded Heart* by Gladys Hunt. Copyright © 1991 by Gladys Hunt. Published by Discovery House Publishers. Used by permission of the author.

28. Slightly adapted from *The Christian's Secret of a Happy Life* by Hannah Whitall Smith. Grosset and Dunlap, no date.

29. Taken from *The Perfect Christian* by Tony Evans. Copyright © 1998 by Tony Evans. W

Publishing Group, Nashville, Tennessee. All rights reserved. Used by permission of the publisher.

30. Taken from *Becoming: Your Self in the Making*. Copyright © 1987 by Calvin Miller. Published by Fleming H. Revell. Used by permission of the author.

31. Taken from *She Can Laugh at the Days to Come* by Valerie Bell. Copyright © 1996 by Valerie Bell. Used by permission of Zondervan.

32. Taken from *On Being a Servant of God* by Warren Wiersbe. Copyright © 1998 by Warren W. Wiersbe. Used by permission of Thomas Nelson Publishers.

33. Reprinted from *Knowing the Face of God*. Copyright © 1996 by Tim Stafford. Used by permission of NavPress, Colorado Springs, CO. All rights reserved. For copies call (800) 366-7788.

34. Taken from *Against the Night* by Charles Colson, Copyright © 1989 by Fellowship Communications. Published by Servant Publications, Box 8617, Ann Arbor, Michigan, 48107. Used with permission of the publisher.

35. Taken from *Finding God* by Larry Crabb Jr. Copyright © 1993 by Lawrence J. Crabb Jr., PhD, PA, dba, Institute of Biblical Counseling. Used by permission of Zondervan.

Closing Prayer. Taken from *Opening Windows* (sound recording). Copyright © 1998 Here to Him Music. Used by permission of Here to Him Music.